WHEREFORE DIDST THOU DOUBT?

A CAREGIVER'S STORY

PATTI EPPERSON

Text and photos copyright © 2018 Patti Epperson.
All rights reserved.
ISBN 978-1983432316

This material is neither made, provided, approved, nor endorsed by Intellectual Reserve, Inc. or The Church of Jesus Christ of Latter-day Saints. Any content or opinions expressed, implied or included in or with the material are solely those of the owner and not those of Intellectual Reserve, Inc. or The Church of Jesus Christ of Latter-day Saints.

Trial of Hope . . . Last Hill and *Liberty Jail, Winter* paintings © Al Rounds. Used with permission.

Lyrics from "Family Can Be Together Forever" used with permission. Lyrics © Ruth Muir Gardner.

Cover and interior design by Kristy G. Stewart of Looseleaf Editorial & Production.

TABLE OF CONTENTS

Prologue	1
Chapter 1	4
Chapter 2	15
Chapter 3	31
Chapter 4	45
Chapter 5	62
Chapter 6	76
Chapter 7	90
Chapter 8	104
Chapter 9	114
Chapter 10	127
Chapter 11	139
Endnotes	150
Acknowledgments	152

PROLOGUE

For God so loved the world that he gave his only begotten
Son, that whoever believeth in him should not perish,
but have everlasting life.

JOHN 3:16

FIRST, I NEED TO explain who God truly is.

He is literally our Father, our Heavenly Father. The Father of our spirits. He wants more than anything for us to return to live with Him. It's comforting to know that our Father is a God. Yet, He is also bound by laws; laws we all must obey. We must choose if we want to return to Him; and we also need to be better to return to Him.

Our spiritual mission on this earth is to grow and become better. We understand this logically: the idea that we need to grow spiritually. And all of us understand physical growth, as well as the pain and discomfort that comes with it. Why would it surprise us that spiritual growth might also include discomfort and pain?

Just as we understand the need for the pain that comes from physical growth, we need to understand it will happen when we grow spiritually, as well. How does a loving Heavenly Father help our spirits grow? How do we ultimately prove that we choose Heavenly Father, no matter what? How do we grow or develop our faith in Him and in ourselves?

Our loving Heavenly Father provided a way for us to succeed. First and foremost, He gave us a Savior. We will always fall short, but our Heavenly Father, in His love and mercy, provided a Savior to give us a way to overcome our weakness. Through our Savior, we can ultimately return to His presence and live with our Heavenly Father forever.

He also gave us other tools: scriptures, prayer, commandments, the Holy Ghost, prophets and leaders, and families to help us grow, love, and serve. All these aid us in becoming more like Him and our Savior.

Are we able to see the big picture? Are we able to have faith in this great plan? Do we truly believe our Heavenly Father wants us to return and live with Him again? Do we really believe He is a God of love? Do we believe He wants us to be happy as much as—and often more than—*we* want to be happy?

I'm sharing my story because this is a real life example of: first, how much Heavenly Father loves each and every one of us, and second, how, with the help of our Savior, we can follow the plan He laid out that will lead to our eternal happiness. No matter how weak or helpless you may be, you can do anything with the Lord's help. Trust me, I'm not unique or amazing, just ask my family and friends or anyone who knows me. But I can't keep silent on how the Lord delivered my family and me. I must proclaim to all who will listen that our Heavenly Father is real and He loves us! Our Savior, Jesus Christ, is real and through His grace, atonement and love, He strengthened me beyond my imagination. If I hadn't relied on my

Savior, especially during this trial, I wouldn't have grown and become a better person. I wouldn't have become the person Heavenly Father knew I could grow to become.

I also want to make it clear that this story is from my point of view. This is how I remembered and processed certain events. I now have ten years of growth and perspective, and that will show in my perspective, as well. Humans are imperfect creatures, so I ask for your patience if I got details wrong or interpreted situations differently than others might have.

I'm thankful my Heavenly Father loved me enough to hurt me, so that I could get to know Him and become a better person and a better daughter of God!

CHAPTER 1

December 2007

Believe in God; believe that he is, and that he created all things, both in heaven and in earth; believe that he has all wisdom, and all power, both in heaven and in earth; believe that man doth not comprehend all the things which the Lord can comprehend.

Mosiah 4:9

One night, years before cancer was even a possibility, Rob had a nightmare. I remember being asleep beside him and waking up to the unfamiliar sound of crying.

It was my husband—sobbing in his sleep. I woke him up, still disoriented from sleep myself, and tried to comfort him as he transitioned back to wakefulness.

"I just had the worst dream ever," he told me, wiping at his wet cheeks. "Our son, Robbie was still a baby and I was carrying him up these unfamiliar stairs. I knew . . . these people were going to sacrifice him. Robbie was looking up at me with his big blue eyes, so full of trust and love for me." Rob paused and shuddered. "I pleaded with them; begged them. Take me instead. Let me be the sacrifice instead."

WHEREFORE DIDST THOU DOUBT?

Summer 1998 Washington DC: Robbie and Rob

It was at that point in the dream when I woke him up.

Two years later, Rob got sick. I always remembered that night; that dream. Rob didn't cry easily and he rarely dreamed so the nightmare stood out in sharp contrast to our usual routine of restful nights. It shook him so thoroughly that he never forgot it: the dream or that awful feeling of being forced to sacrifice his beloved child.

I used to think that challenges and trials came about when you didn't follow the teachings of Christ. I believed with all my heart that if I always stayed on the strait and narrow path, i.e. kept the commandments of God, I'd never have trials in my life. I thought those kinds of problems were simply brought about by making the wrong choices.

When I heard Elder Dallin H. Oaks, a General Authority for the Church of Jesus Christ of Latter-day Saints, speak about how "opposition permits us to grow toward what our Heavenly Father would have us become,"[1] I thought "opposition" simply meant choosing the Lord instead of the world—avoiding inappropriate entertainment, saying no to drugs and alcohol, avoiding immodest clothing. *That* was opposition. Therefore, if I kept the commandments, my life would be easy.

I didn't understand the scripture found in the Book of Mormon, 2 Nephi 2:11, which reads, "For it must needs be, that there is an opposition in all things. If not so, . . . righteousness could not be brought to pass, neither wickedness, neither holiness nor misery, neither good nor bad. Wherefore, all things must needs be a compound in one; wherefore, if it should be one body it must needs remain as dead, having no life neither death, nor corruption nor incorruption, happiness nor misery, neither sense nor insensibility."

The last day I was still under the blissful delusion that any trials I faced were under my control was a rainy

Halloween 2007: Rob and I

Wherefore Didst Thou Doubt?

Summer 2007 McCall, Idaho: Ellie (6), me (32), John (10 months), Rob (34), Luke (10 months), Robbie (10) and Jake (8)

Tuesday in December. It was two weeks before Christmas and my husband, Rob, had a match with his indoor soccer team. His game began just as the aerobics class I taught ended. For ten minutes, our five children (Robbie, 11; Jake, 8; Ellie, almost 7; and the twins, Luke and John, 14 months) would be unsupervised, sitting on the stadium stands as the soccer game started. I felt a thrill as I rushed into the arena, my damp clothes clinging to me because I didn't have time to change after working out and my short hair glistening with sweat. We were busy, at times even frantic, but we were happy and the familiar smells of rubber turf and sweat were the smells of many happy memories.

I joined my kids on the stands and cheered for my husband. He made two goals for his team and they walked away with another victory. We came home tired but glowing. We prodded our tired kids into their beds, then settled into our own bed to half-watch the news

Fall 2007 Vancouver, Washington: Rob playing indoor soccer

and chat about the next day. He had a flight from our home in Portland to Spokane, Washington for a work party, he reminded me as he ate his favorite bedtime snack of Chips Ahoy and milk.

We fell asleep and closed out another busy but average day. I didn't know then how sacred such a mundane day could be. The next morning, everything changed.

Rob woke up sick. He was throwing up and his head hurt. The flu had already made the rounds in our home the week before. It was no major leap to assume Rob was only the latest victim. He canceled his trip to Spokane and tried to suffer through the symptoms.

Thursday night, he had two of his friends from church come over to give him blessing, a special prayer in our religion that involves making a request for help from the Lord. One of them, Jayson, was a newer member to our church and didn't feel very comfortable about giving a blessing, but Rob still insisted he do it. The blessing said Rob would return to family, work, and church assignments. I felt comforted when the prayer ended, assured that eventually life would return to normal.

By Friday, Rob wasn't getting better. His head throbbed and he couldn't keep food or medicine down. When your child is sick, it's normal to attend to every ache and pain, every need. But husbands are different and I wasn't sure how worried to be. Rob was tough, not prone to complaining, so I knew something was really wrong when he asked me to call his mother, Adrienne, who was a nurse, and ask her if he needed to see a doctor.

I remember telling her over the phone, "He can't keep any medicine down and his head is killing him. He's in so much pain. Is it dehydration?"

She told us to go to the emergency room and get an IV put in. The morning was a blur as I got the older children ready and off to school and arranged for a friend to come watch the twins. When we arrived at the hospital, the doctors said Rob was suffering from a migraine. They gave him medicine through an IV and sent us home. Because of the medicine, Rob was finally able to sleep for the first time in three days.

At this point, my life still felt normal and my usual routine still possible. I put the twins down for a nap and left them with my sleeping, but seemingly on the mend, husband. I needed to fulfill my volunteer duties at the elementary school where my kids attended. I'd promised to grade some papers and I thought I was still living in a universe where promises like this could easily be kept.

By dinnertime that night, the medicine from the emergency room had run

Thanksgiving 2007 McCall, Idaho: Rob holding John

its course through Rob's system. He awoke to the same symptoms that had led us to the ER that morning. I called Adrienne again, wondering if there was more we could do.

"I think if you go to the ER twice in 24 hours, you don't have to pay them another co-pay," she said.

Rob was sick and I was worried, so we decided to go back to the hospital. I was once again forced to leave my children in the hands of friends and I thought sadly that my husband would probably not be able to take Robbie on his first scout campout they'd been planning for the coming weekend. I still held out hope that Rob would at least be feeling better by Ellie's birthday party the next day.

The doctors ran some tests. Then they ran some more. They couldn't figure out what was wrong—they had no idea what to do or how to control his pain. By one a.m., Saturday morning, they finally admitted Rob. I remember all I had with me was my purse. I'd never expected it to take this long; it didn't occur to me to pack a bag of supplies, or arrange extended childcare.

In a fog, I arranged for my friends to run Ellie's seventh birthday party. I was able to stop by for an hour during the party to give her a hug and wish her happy birthday, but my mind was back at the hospital, with Rob. It was my daughter's birthday! In our family, birthdays are a really big deal! It is that person's special day and everything that day revolved around the birthday person. My little Ellie saw her mom run into the house, completely distracted, wish her a happy birthday and run out the door again. The mom guilt and wife guilt were in battle. I wanted to be there for Ellie, but no one was there for Rob. Thank goodness I had amazing friends who tried to help Ellie feel special on her birthday, even though her parents could not be there for her.

I changed my clothes, grabbed a laptop and my iPod, and went back to the hospital. I had no idea how long we'd be there. I'd never felt so helpless and useless; the only resource I could offer my husband was waiting beside him and nothing more.

At one point, the doctors thought it might be meningitis, a highly contagious infection that causes headaches, fever, sensitivity to light, and muscular rigidity. We kept the lights off and made sure Rob's room was always dark and quiet. That meant my children and the family that had helped babysit them needed to be quarantined until it was ruled out and so, for the first time in their lives, my kids got to have a sleepover.

I settled into a corner bed-window seat and turned on old general conference talks because it was the only thing I could listen to, what with the constant interruptions from nurses and the insistent hums and beeps of all the machines Rob was hooked up to.

Sunday morning dawned and still no answers, though they'd been able to rule out meningitis. As wonderful as my friends were to babysit all weekend, they had children of their own and I was going to need more than a little help with mine. I was torn between being by my husband's side and being home with my children. I couldn't be both places at once. I knew the best person to be with Rob was his mom. Plus her being a nurse was a bonus. I called her and asked if she could come help. She jumped on a plane that night and flew to Oregon from Utah. She immediately offered to stay at Rob's bedside so I could go home and spend some time with the children.

As a mom of five kids, running the family schedule and keeping everyone on task was one of my primary responsibilities. I felt it was important to have the kids' lives stay as normal as possible. I usually run a very tight ship, but I couldn't plan more than a moment or two ahead because I was stuck between two universes: one where I knew what was going to happen next and this new one, where all I could do was wait for someone else to give me some answers. I did the only thing a mom can do when everything is up in the air—I made a plan for the next day. My friend, Jennifer would come over after she chaperoned a school field trip to watch my twins so I could return to the hospital. The field trip, which included my oldest son, Robbie, was at a senior center. The students sang Christmas carols to the elderly. While they were there, Jennifer got a call from my mother-in-law, asking her to please rush to my house as soon as she could because they had some news and I was needed at the hospital.

When she arrived at my door, I was surprised to see her earlier than we'd planned.

"They have an answer," she told me. "They know what is wrong. You need to get to the hospital as soon as possible."

Feeling worried but hopeful, I rushed to leave. As I was turning out of our neighborhood, I saw Robbie's fifth grade class walking down the street, returning from their field trip. I waved to all the students, my eyes scanning the group for my son.

I finally spotted him at the very back, his shoulders hunched, his cheeks wet with tears. I threw my car in park, jumped out, and rushed to his side, wrapping my arms around him.

"Is Dad dead?" he asked with a shaky voice.

I swallowed hard and began to cry. "No, no, Dad isn't dead," I said in a hushed voice.

Robbie told me he saw Jennifer during the field trip get a phone call and then rush out of the room crying, and he'd assumed the worst.

I held him closer and murmured into his hair, "It's okay. The doctors know what's wrong and I'm on my way to find out right now."

I told his teacher I was taking him with me, then I dropped him off at home before heading to the hospital. I'd spent the weekend at this hospital and I knew it like the back of my hand. I ran up the back stairs and headed straight to the familiar room. I opened the door, excited to have an answer. The first thing I noticed when I walked into Rob's hospital room was that the lights were on and he was sitting up in bed. My heart fluttered with excitement and I felt light and hopeful for the first time in almost a week. I turned to look at my husband, the beginnings of a smile on my face.

Our eyes met. My smile fell away and my knees buckled. I knew the news was bad. I'd never seen that look in his eyes before. They were sad, lost, and cried out three words: "I'm so sorry."

I grabbed the doorframe to keep myself upright, but inside, I could feel myself beginning to collapse. Adrienne was suddenly at my side, holding me up. With her hands grasping my arms, she whispered fiercely in my ear, "You be strong for him. You. Be. Strong."

I stood tall, took a deep breath and walked over to Rob. Without a word, I hugged him. He collapsed into sobs, muttering, "I'm sorry, I'm sorry," over and over again as the tears fell.

Soon after, they gave my worst fears a name. It was Stage 4 Cancer.

CHAPTER 2

December 2007

*Our Heavenly Father . . . knows that we learn and grow
and become stronger as we face and survive the
trials through which we must pass.*

Prophet Thomas S. Monson[2]

It had only been a week. Last Tuesday, I was sitting on the bleachers with my five children, cheering for Rob as he scored a soccer goal. This Tuesday, I was sitting in a hospital room, blinking against the bright fluorescent lights as I tried to come to terms with my new reality. What was I supposed to do now? How could I keep living the busy life I'd been living while taking care of a husband with cancer? How much would my daily life change now? Did I have the strength to be there for Rob as much as he was going to need me?

Rob wasn't worried about himself. He wasn't angry at an unfeeling universe. He didn't complain about getting dealt an unfair hand. He only asked, "What should I do? What can I do?"

His soccer team came over to visit him after their game. Rob was happy and upbeat with them, asking

Monday December 17, 2007 Vancouver, Washington: The day we found out Rob had stage 4 cancer, Rob, Robbie, Ellie, Luke, John, Adrienne (Rob's mom) and Jake

about the game and what he'd missed. He couldn't wait to get back out on the field with them and play again.

He wrote a letter to our extended family and friends soon after to give them a glimpse into what he was thinking:

> *It reminds me of one of my favorite stories in 3rd Nephi. The righteous people have been awaiting the miracle of the Savior's birth. They waited "steadfastly" without murmur. The night was now at hand, the Savior was to be born that very next day—or they would be put to death. How does one handle that? What do you tell your children that evening when you prepare for bed? Do you beg for your life and that of your loved ones?*
>
> *As Nephi prayed for his people, he heard the Lord tell him to "Lift up his head and be of good cheer . . .*

on the morrow come I into the world." I doubt sweeter words had ever been uttered to Nephi! What an answer to a simply heartfelt prayer. Never did he ask, "Can Thou change this or that?" Simply, "Please help us know what to do."

As I look at my family and where we go from here, I think of those simple things. What does The Lord need us to learn? Are we willing to do it?

The doctors sent us home a couple of days later. While we had a preliminary diagnosis, we still didn't know what type of cancer it was—lymphoma or melanoma—and further tests needed to be done. In the back of my mind, I remembered the blessing given to him before we knew it was cancer. I felt that if my faith in Christ was strong enough, the blessing would be fulfilled.

December 19, 2007: Rob and his brother/best friend Andy, who flew in as soon as he could. Rob is keeping up on his work!

We also still didn't know what was causing his painful headaches, but still—hope burned in my chest. Yes, his diagnosis was scary but now we knew what beast to slay and someday—I just knew it—our lives would return to normal.

With Rob home and resting, and cancer treatments on a distant horizon, I set my mind to more immediate matters. I hadn't done much Christmas shopping, even though the holiday was a week away. I sat my kids down and tried to explain to them that, because of our current situation, we wouldn't be doing some of our normal traditions. First and foremost we would not be going to Utah for Christmas to visit family. Ellie and I wouldn't be going with aunts and cousins to see the Nutcracker. And there was no time to play the game, "What is Santa going to bring me?" I needed a list of toys they wanted, and I needed it now.

I stumbled over my words, trying to say things as gently as I could. It felt like I was telling them, "Your dad has cancer, there's no Santa Clause; what do you want for Christmas? I'm going to Target in ten minutes."

Christmas is my favorite time of the year. I usually spend many hours trying to find the perfect present for each one of my children. But this year, Christmas was ruined!

It turns out that the Christmas spirit is a limited resource and most of my energy, my heart, and my tears were now spent in hospital rooms and on phone calls with family members; I literally had nothing left to keep the magic of Christmas aglow. But I doubt my kids would've noticed the shimmer anyway. They were just as heartsick and worried as me.

My friend, Jennifer, came with me to Target. I wandered the aisles in a fog. I blinked against harsher fluorescent lighting, noticing how it cast the linoleum floors in a similar sickly yellow as the floors in the hallways of the hospital. I looked at the other shoppers, almost accusingly, wondering how they could walk around like everything was normal, like the world made sense. Who cares if Princess Sparkle Pony was on sale last week but not now and you don't have a coupon; my husband has cancer. How can you argue about whether to get the blue Ninja Turtle or the red one; my husband has cancer. Don't snap at the woman who accidentally bumped you with her cart, because it doesn't matter! My husband has cancer!

"Okay, Patti, who are we doing first?" Jennifer said, forcing me to focus.

I named a child and she pulled out the accompanying list, then pushed me forward. Like this, with robotic motions and Jennifer's gentle but firm prodding, I made it through all five children. My cart filled up but my brain was still foggy and my heart ached. For the first time since having kids, I didn't once giggle with excitement over finding the perfect gift. I didn't pause to imagine a tender, little face lighting up at a new toy. The only gift I *wanted* to give them was beyond my ability: a healthy father.

Christmas morning arrived on schedule and somehow there were brightly wrapped gifts piled under the tree. When I woke up, I could see that Rob wasn't feeling well. I refused to start the holiday without him so I ushered all the children into the twins' bedroom, turned on a TV show, and waited.

Christmas 2007: Rob is talking to his family in Utah

We could hear him, through the wall, throwing up in the master bathroom. I don't know what my kids were thinking; I was afraid to ask them. We sat in silence, the only noise coming from the helium-voiced cartoon characters on the TV in front of us, as we pretended like this was a normal way to spend Christmas morning.

When he felt well enough to come downstairs with us, the first thing he did was apologize for making us wait. I couldn't believe it. He was so sick but he didn't complain. He only worried about us.

If you look back at the pictures from that day, we look like a normal, happy family. One of my favorites is of Rob with his head thrown back, laughing, as he talks on the phone with his siblings. You can't tell in the photo that he had a burst blood vessel under his left eye from throwing up.

On New Year's Eve, we got together with some friends and rented a room at a local hotel so the kids could swim at their indoor pool. I was scrambling to keep the excited kids in line as we made our way down the hotel hallway toward the pool. I looked back to check on Rob and noticed he could barely walk. He was trying to hold himself together because he wanted the kids to have a good time but he had to grip the wall and pull himself forward on unsteady feet. He could barely hold himself up or move.

It was shortly after this that we finally admitted to ourselves something was really wrong and we couldn't sit back and wait for the cancer test results. Rob was in constant pain; he was becoming less coherent, less able to move. As much as I'd come to hate that section of the hospital, I realized I needed to take Rob back to the ER.

I was a 32-year-old housewife but now suddenly, I had to be a medical advocate for my husband. I told the nurses and the doctors, "Something is *wrong.*" Even as they tried to reassure me and give me easy answers or put me off, I insisted. I pleaded. I explained.

"I know my husband. I know how he acts and how he

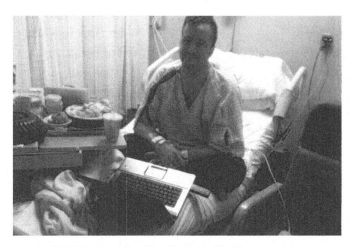

January 3, 2008: Rob working from his hospital bed

reacts and something is wrong," I insisted and insisted. Finally, the doctors realized he had cancer cells in his spinal fluid. These cancer cells were getting caught in the little vents that went from his brain to his spine. This was preventing the spinal fluid from draining properly and it was putting pressure on his head.

We found ourselves being readmitted to the hospital so Rob could have a shunt put in his brain to drain all the excess spinal fluid into his belly area. I was relieved to finally have an answer and a solution to Rob's extreme suffering. But when he awoke from the surgery, we were in for a new shock.

He couldn't move his legs.

Less than a month earlier, he was scoring soccer goals. Now they were fitting him for a wheelchair. Though the surgery was a success, the pressure build-up on Rob's brain, along with his weight loss and the fact that he'd been bedridden for almost three weeks, caused the loss of movement in his legs. Doctors were hopeful that the paralysis would not be permanent because he had some feeling and movement. Though he couldn't stand or get into his wheelchair without help, we knew we just needed to be patient and wait until he could get his strength back.

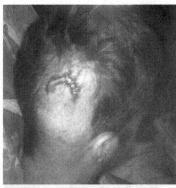

January 5, 2008: Shunt that was put into Rob's head to relieve the spinal fluid, which was causing pressure on his brain, therefore the throwing up and pain.

Some good came from the surgery, though. Using nodes from Rob's stomach, the doctors were able to take a biopsy and confirm the type of cancer he had: melanoma. We were relieved to have confirmation, and relieved that he wouldn't need to go through another surgery for the time being.

January 5, 2008: family visiting Rob after his surgery

I wrote on our family blog a few days later:

> *We just got back from the doctor's and the labs are back! He does have cancer and the type is melanoma. Dr. Liss said that it's advanced and very serious. She did say that the top expert in melanoma cancer lives in Portland. We have an appointment with him (Dr. Walter Urba) next Wednesday, at which time we'll talk about our treatment plans.*
>
> *Dr. Liss said that Rob's treatment will be very strenuous and very aggressive. We thank everyone for their prayers and ask everyone to keep on praying for us and also Dr. Urba, that he will be enlightened to know the correct way to treat Rob. I know the Lord is hearing everyone's prayers!*

"Do you know how to work a wheelchair?" the physical therapist asked me soon after the diagnosis came in. I was being trained on how to care for a paraplegic: how to get Rob in and out of the car, up and down stairs, in and out of bed.

"I'm pretty good with a double stroller," I said, eyeing the contraption in front of me. I'd seen plenty of wheelchairs in my life but I'd never really *looked* at one before.

The physical therapist laughed. "This will be a little different."

I nodded in understanding. "Different" was the only thing that was constant in my life right now. The only guarantee I had was that our lives would be different. Even at my house, different was the new normal. Despite all the time I was currently spending with Rob at the hospital, I still had five children at home who needed to be cared for. So our families set up a plan—parents, siblings, aunts, and grandmothers all took turns coming to watch the kids, flying in like angels. Each week, there was another family member there to help. I don't even know how they did it. I just knew my kids were being well cared for, allowing me to give all of my attention to Rob.

Soon after the surgery, the doctors became worried that Rob's progress was getting worse, not better, so they took an MRI of his spine. They discovered cancer cells were putting pressure on his spinal cord and pinching off the nerves to his legs. He could feel everything, all the way down to his toes, but his legs tingled from mid-thigh down.

This was Tuesday. It seemed bad news always came on Tuesdays. The next day, they began radiation on his spine, and Thursday he began taking chemo medication. Rob and I joked that it was like being at a hospital camp: he got a schedule every morning telling him where to

WHEREFORE DIDST THOU DOUBT?

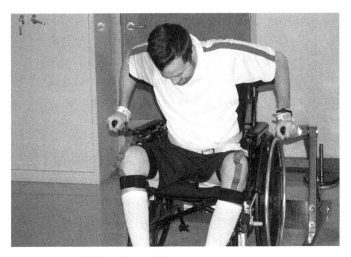

Rob doing his wheelchair physical therapy.

be and what time to be there. They were going to focus on the cells in his spine and once they eradicated those, there was a chance he'd be able to move his legs again. Rob settled into physical therapy, learning the art of the wheelchair and how to move his body with its new limitations. It was busy, but I liked being busy and every task he did—physical therapy, chemo, radiation treatments—meant we were closer to coming back home.

In the hospital, there was a large meeting room that the patients' families could use. We took advantage of the space to keep up our tradition of weekly Family Home Evenings (FHE); one night a week where our family gets together and has a short gospel lesson followed by a fun activity.

I wrote about one such evening on our family blog:

> *Last night was so much fun! Grandma Sheri made roast, mashed potatoes, and Yorkshire pudding! The kids and I came for dinner, sat around the table and*

had a normal family dinner (minus the twins). Jake then taught the lesson for FHE and we had some blonde brownie (which we shared with the nurses). It's nice to be in this big room, so the kids can come and visit and not get too bored. This morning, we worked on more practical things, like getting a wheelchair up the stairs and getting on the toilet. I had the biggest workout of the day, with the wheelchair and stairs! We know this is all getting us closer to getting Rob home. They said he might be coming home later this week! I took some pictures of his physical therapy for everyone to see some of the things he's working on. We are so amazed by all the acts of support from everyone. It's great to know there are so many people out there who care for Rob!

Love,
Patti

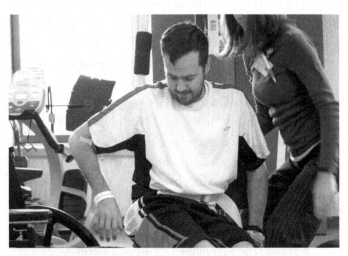

Rob and I learning how to transfer him in and out of his wheelchair

Almost every article of clothing Rob owned had BYU (Brigham Young University) on it, which would often inspire questions from hospital staff, much to Rob's delight. He loved talking about his alma mater and the church behind it. I brought his computer in and he worked as much as he could.

Rob's lower muscles began to respond to the treatments. I remember giving him a foot massage one night and he started wiggling his other foot. We laughed with delight and I marveled at how such a simple moment could mean this much to us. Everything meant we were one step closer to going home.

We began to settle in and accept that this crazy, somewhat nomadic life filled with nurses and doctors and physical therapists and visiting family was our new normal.

On January 16, Rob wrote another email to his family:

> *All in all, it has been a really surreal time. I am not sure what I expected, and I think I did not expect anything at the same time. Who has any idea why something like this happens, or what you do with it, or what you are supposed to do with it? I think I have come to the conclusion that I will figure it out today, tomorrow, or the next day. My Dad asked me a while ago, why did this happen to me, not him, not someone else? I think it came down to this. WHY NOT ME? It is not the actual experience but what the experience will teach us ALL about life and our relationship with one another, our Savior, Our Father in Heaven; and what we do in those relationships and how do we make people's lives better.*

That was his attitude. Not "why me?" but "why *not* me?" He said, "What makes me any better than anyone else? What makes me deserve to escape this trial when someone else would not?"

In 1995, Elder Richard G. Scott gave a talk on this very issue: "To ask, 'Why does this have to happen to me? Why do I have to suffer this, now? What have I done to cause this?' will lead you into blind alleys. It really does no good to ask questions that reflect opposition to the will of God. Rather ask, 'What am I to do? What am I to learn from this experience? What am I to change? Whom am I to help? How can I remember my many blessings in times of trial?'"[3]

During this time, I was fortunate to have a wise bishop—the man in charge of overseeing our congregation—who kept me in my calling as a Gospel Doctrine teacher. Anyone else would've looked at my life, seen that I was barely functioning, and released me. And it wasn't a biweekly or monthly calling. In my church, I was expected to teach a scripture-focused lesson every Sunday for an adult Sunday School class. But I loved it. I loved teaching and the calling forced me to be in my scriptures every day. It forced me to spend some of my time focused on something other than my immediate trials. I had to take time out and think of others. I had to ponder the scriptures. I couldn't just sit and dwell on the trials in front of me.

During one of my sessions scouring the scriptures, I came across Mosiah, Chapter 24 and it struck me in a way it never had before.

> *14 And I will also ease the burdens which are put upon your shoulders, that even you cannot feel them upon your backs, even while you are in bondage; and this will I do that ye may stand as witnesses for me hereafter, and that ye may know of a surety that I, the Lord God, do visit my people in their afflictions.*
>
> *15 And now it came to pass that the burdens which were laid upon Alma and his brethren were made light; yea, **the Lord did strengthen them that they could bear up their burdens with ease**, and they did **submit cheerfully and with patience to all the will of the Lord.***
>
> *21 Yea, and in the valley of Alma they poured out their thanks to God because he had been merciful unto them, and eased their burdens . . . and none could deliver them except it were the Lord their God.*

I also remembered a quote from Elder David A. Bednar. "[The Lord] can reach out, touch, succor, heal, and strengthen us to be more than we could ever be and help us to do that which we could never do relying only upon our own power."[4]

I could see and feel the Lord strengthening me. But how could I submit *cheerfully* and *patiently*? How could I be cheerful when my husband couldn't walk? How could I be cheerful with a diagnosis of cancer? How could I be cheerful when my whole life had been turned completely upside down?

After some prayer and pondering, the answer came to me. I realized I needed gratitude. Rob's attitude toward everything that was happening to him was: "What are we going to learn from this? How can I be an example to everyone I come in contact with?" We lived outside of Portland and were in a unique situation. As a young family with lots of kids, we were a bit of a curiosity to those around us. People were intrigued by our little family, which led to many opportunities to share our testimonies; we were able to bear witness to everything the Lord was doing for us.

At first, I didn't realize the Lord was strengthening me so much. But I came to realize that *this* was the enabling power of the atonement of Jesus Christ. Before, I simply understood the atonement of Jesus Christ as something we used in the process of seeking forgiveness for sins. But I didn't understand that it was also meant to strengthen us.

Without Christ, there's no way I would've been able to get through this trial. I didn't realize it, but all those years I'd spent building a relationship of trust with Christ by studying my scriptures and exercising my faith enabled me to use the atonement of Christ when I needed it.

When the trial comes, you can't suddenly depend on the Lord if you haven't already built a relationship with Him. If you've spent every day running a mile, then when it comes time to run for your life, your body will know what to do. If you've spent every day trusting the Lord and building a relationship with Him, then when it comes time to put your life in the Lord's hands, your spirit will know what to do.

CHAPTER 3

January 2008

God does notice us, and he wathces over us. But it is usually through another person that he meets our needs.

Prophet Spencer W. Kimball[5]

Now that Rob had been fitted for the wheelchair and I'd been trained on how to help him use it, we only needed a final okay from the doctor to move him home. With the shunt in his head, Rob was virtually pain free and back to his old self, for the most part. Though taking care of Rob was definitely easier at the hospital, where everything he needed was a nurse call-button away, we missed the kids desperately. They were excited to hear that Daddy would be home soon, they didn't even mind giving up their playroom so he could have a bedroom on the main floor.

On January 16, 2008, Rob wrote on our family blog:

I figured I might as well type something on here for you all to read and update you on my thoughts and deep ponderings. I'm not sure I've had that many but I will try and be profound and life-altering here.

Not really. I used to be a lot more insightful, I think. Certain things have a way of changing one's insight.

I really want to thank everyone for the support; it's inspiring, the support the emails, calls, and visits. It truly gives me a small sense of what the word FAMILY means. I'm not sure I truly know what to do with it all. When I think about it, I usually break down and cry.

We just found out that on Friday they will map out the radiation that they will do for the cancer near my menigie (SP), near my spine. This is a good sign; this means that what we've been doing near my lower spine is working and allowing us to progress now to the brain, which is where the main problem is located. We probably have a weekish left on the current radiation, then a few weeks on the new area.

Also, I found out that after they do my brain mapping, which obviously will take hours, on Friday I will get to come HOME!!!! Not sure what that means, no nurses for food, making beds, etc. Good though. Home will just be nice. I'm a little nervous, but excited. I know the kids will be happy. Plus my room has no ESPN, TNT, or really anything for that matter.

Thank you for everything
Rob

However, we soon found out Rob's excitement to go home was a bit premature.

"How's everybody doing?" Doctor Liss asked as she strode into Rob's hospital room.

I smiled up at her. "We're good! Excited to go home today."

"Actually, we can't release him until your home is wheelchair accessible," Doctor Liss said.

My mouth dropped open. I pressed my lips closed to keep me from shouting out the obvious question: "Why didn't you tell me that a week ago!?" Instead, I nodded. "Okay. What do we need to do for that?"

Beside me, in his hospital bed, I heard Rob chuckle and I knew he could tell I'd bitten back my first response.

Doctor Liss walked us through the process of getting a home "wheelchair ready" and my mind reeled at this new challenge in front of me. It was Friday afternoon. I'd been naïve to hope we'd be home for the weekend, but now I had to figure out how to organize, pay for and execute a home renovation project.

It was just after 5 p.m. when I hit "send" on an email addressed to the leadership of my church congregation. I told them we needed our home wheelchair ready and if they had any help or advice for me, I'd really appreciate it.

By 8 p.m., my dad called to say there were men from the church in our yard, measuring the front steps so they could put in a ramp.

At 7 a.m. the next morning, the same group was busily installing all the necessary parts to make our home safe for Rob: a ramp at the front door, a new bathroom door, a bar in the bathtub. It was a stormy weekend, but the rainy Portland skies didn't slow them down.

My dad told them he'd be happy to pay for all the costs but every last man waved the offer away. They all said the same thing—at some point Rob had done something for each of them and they were happy for a chance to repay him in some way. My husband's naturally kind and

January 12, 2008: I emailed two people from my congregation Friday night at 5 p.m. and explained how the doctor's would not let us go home until our home was wheel chair acceptable. This picture was taken the very next day, Saturday morning at 8 am!

generous personality was bearing fruit now, serving him well in his time of need.

Doctor Liss came back to our room the following afternoon to check on Rob. I mentioned that our home was wheelchair ready and Doctor Liss stared at me in shock.

"I've never heard of a house getting ready that fast," she said, her eyes wide. "I've never seen ramps get put in, in less than 24 hours."

"We have a lot of really good people in our lives," I told her.

She smiled and nodded. "Then it looks like you guys are ready to go home."

Doctor Liss and the rest of the hospital staff that worked with us expressed their amazement at the huge amount of help we were getting at home. It was hard explaining how our congregation was like our extended family. It made me realize how lucky I was to have a church family. I wondered how anyone could go through an experience like fighting cancer without one.

I was excited to get Rob home. He was exhausted the night before from working his legs, so he went to sleep early. I was nervous and extra attentive to any new pains or different behaviors Rob displayed. I was told to watch for any new symptoms and I was worried something might prevent our trip home.

To my relief, when I arrived the next morning, Rob was smiling and ready for his big day. He had to go through his physical therapy appointments and get mapped for a new round of radiation. He also decided to shave his mustache and I thought he looked so much like a sweet baby, I wanted to kiss him all over his face.

When we drove up to our house, January 18, the first thing we noticed were brightly colored balloons dancing against a grey sky, and a banner spanning the garage that read, "Welcome Home, Rob!"

January 18, 2008: Friends welcoming Rob home! He had been in the hospital since January 2.

Trying to get Rob out of the car for our first time!

Tears sprang to my eyes as we pulled up and I saw the eager faces of my children, family, and friends. As I took in the scene, I knew with my whole heart that I never would have gotten this far without the unselfish service of my friends and family. There was no possible way.

It felt strange coming home with the wheelchair. Having it at the hospital made it seem like something from a different world. But when we brought it home, it made it feel more real. Like bringing home a new baby from the hospital—that moment where reality hits you and you realize, "I'm a parent!" Except this time it was, "I'm the wife of a man in a wheelchair." Yes, it was all too real and a little bit scary. But I had confidence we'd be able to adjust. And even with these new, daunting changes, the fact remained: we were home!

I'd spent almost 24 hours a day at the hospital with Rob. Somehow, my household kept running without me. Someone set up a system so that there was always a family member staying at the house. Everyone was assigned a week and they travelled on their own time and at their own cost. My parents, my siblings, aunts, and uncles all came to help. They asked, "What week? When do you need me?" And to this day, I don't know who arranged all that. I don't even know how they got to and from the airport. It was all just handled. Since most of my physical and psychic energy was focused on Rob at the time, I didn't realize what a miracle this was.

Our kids loved it. They got to spend time with family members that they'd never met or barely saw. It was a perpetual slumber party for them and because most of these relatives were from out of town, they got to play the tour guides and show them all the beauty Portland has to offer.

Jennifer told me later that when she woke up and said her morning prayers, she'd ask, "What does Patti need today?" A lot of times Heavenly Father knew what I was going to need, even though I didn't. She took over carpool duties for me, made sure my household was taken care

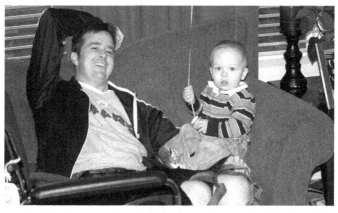

John and Rob. Rob was so happy to finally be home! You can see the straps on his legs, this helped us lift his legs up and move them.

Aunt Caren helping Robbie with his homework

Adrienne and Rob figuring out the bathroom with a wheel chair.

Aunt Liza with the twins

Granna and Shramps with Rob. Granna massaging Rob's legs

Grandma Adrienne and Luke

Aunt Deedee and John

Rob's cousin Tony watching TV with Ellie

of, and always checked in with my kids.

The examples of unselfish service, great and small, are too numerous for me to recount. Whatever our need was, someone was there to help fill it. I remember Rob had to get into the shower and visiting church members helped me carry him upstairs. He was too weak to shower himself and they stepped in, without complaint or murmur, and took care of him. I still have the image of my weakened and humbled husband in the arms of these gentle men. They were so respectful, so honored to be the ones to help him.

We had built a solid foundation in our community, but we never thought as we were giving service that we would need it returned to us a hundredfold like this.

You never know when you're going to be the one in need of service, but when you live your life engaged in service, as Rob did, all of that effort comes back to you. We had visitors all the time. People would come to bring us meals, or massage his feet, or just talk to him.

During this period, Rob was trying to return to some semblance of a

Jennifer and I

normal life. He was working as much as he could and even still attended to his church calling when able. But the radiation treatments were hard and aggressive. The doctors literally had to take him to the edge of death to eradicate the cancer cells. It made him so tired.

The first Sunday with him home, we didn't have church until 3 p.m. I felt confident we had plenty of time to get the family ready. But he was pushing himself a little too hard that day. Around lunchtime, he admitted to us that he knew he wouldn't be able to attend church.

I brought him back to his room and I could see he was bothered. For the first time ever, he expressed his frustration with not feeling well and not being able to do the things he wanted to. It was 20 minutes before church was scheduled to begin when I decided he needed a blessing.

I called two of our closest neighbors who were part of our church congregation to see if they could come give him a blessing but both families had already left for church. I called the church to see if anyone there could come over to give him a blessing. It was our bishop who answered my call and moments later, he was at our front door with another member of our congregation.

Rob was moved by this, especially considering church was about to start. Bishop Hamman talked with us and I sat in awe as I listened to the wonderful words he spoke. He talked of the atonement of our Savior and how much he relies on it daily. Bishop Hamman gave Rob a blessing of comfort. We truly felt the love and support of our Savior and Heavenly Father. In that moment, I could clearly see their hands in our lives, helping us each day.

Some of the service we received was unseen and mysterious. On January 21, 2008, I went to the pharmacy to pick up Rob's chemotherapy pills only to find out they cost $1,500. I didn't have that kind of money readily available, so I told the pharmacy to hold the prescription while I contacted my doctor.

"Are you sure this is right?" I asked her over the phone. "Is this for the whole month? We don't have the money right now."

"Hold off on buying it," she said. "Let me see what I can do."

I felt blessed to have a doctor that took my calls and was attentive and responsive to us.

The next day, I was back at the pharmacy for another prescription and the pharmacy tech reminded me that I had other pills waiting for me.

"We're holding those," I told her. "Until I can figure out how to pay them."

She frowned, confused. "But they're already paid for."

"What?" I asked. "The chemotherapy pills? The $1,500 pills?"

She nodded and handed me the bag. "Yes, it's all taken care of. You just need to take them."

"But who?" I stumbled out the words.

She shrugged and went back to work. I pulled out my cell phone to text Doctor Liss.

Thank you so much for taking care of this! I wrote.

Taking care of what? Doctor Liss answered back soon after.

The chemotherapy pills. How did you get the insurance to cover it all?

I don't know what you're talking about, came the reply. *I haven't had a chance to look into that yet.*

I stared at the text message, mystified. Then stared at the medicine in my hands. To this day, I still don't know what happened.

A lot of the service we received included words of support and love, as well as the heartfelt prayers of friends and family.

We tried to get back to our normal lives as much as we could, which included going to Institute (or bible study) classes. Even though Rob was often tired and sick, he made every effort to go when he could. It was during this time that I received a letter from our Institute teacher.

Dear Patti,

I was so excited to see you and Rob in Institute today. Every single lesson I have prepared the last few weeks has been with you and Rob in my mind. I shared a few of the details with the class, because many of them have gotten to know you through approximately four years of class, and have heard and felt your testimony. They were praying for you and Rob each week. I was sad at first that you had to go to Rob's appointment before we got to the uplifting part of the lesson, but then I realized that the both of you didn't come today to be taught—you came to teach.

The spirit in the room after you left was so powerful, because we saw a modern day Joseph and his wife, doing the best they can to keep their covenants and be steadfast and immovable. I know in the middle of the night, things can look dark, but your faith and optimism as you wait on the Lord have been remarkable. The timing for Rob's life is in the Lord's hands as it was for Joseph and because he is a perfect and just God and a merciful God also, his timing in your life will be perfect also. Thank you for your examples. We love you and will continue to pray for you. With all my heart and prayers,

Sandy Ririe

A few days later, I had to take my oldest son, Robbie, to a special event for our church. He was 11 and would be turning 12 the following December. That's a big milestone in our religion for young men because they are given special spiritual responsibilities. On January 27, 2008 there was a meeting to teach the 11, soon-to-be 12 year olds about their coming responsibilities. It broke my heart a bit that I was the one to take Robbie, instead of Rob. He was the only boy there without his father and I was feeling a little sorry for him. For myself. For Rob. Then I got a text from my dad.

President Gordon B. Hinkley had just passed away. He'd served as the prophet of our church for 13 years. For the first time since Rob was diagnosed with cancer, I wasn't thinking about Rob or our sad situation.

Rob, Jake, and Robbie at the Salt Lake Temple visitor's center

My heart ached for President Hinkley. I knew he would be greatly missed and it brought home for me the fact that even though my family's suffering was very real and very deep, we weren't the only ones with major trials. It was sad that Rob couldn't sit beside his son at this meeting, but he was waiting for us at home and really, we had much to be grateful for.

CHAPTER 4

FEBRUARY 2008

Come unto me, all ye that labour and are heavy laden, and I will give you rest. Take my yoke upon you, and learn of me; for I am meek and lowly in heart; and ye shall find rest unto your souls. For my yoke is easy, and my burden is light.

MATTHEW 11:28–30

FEBRUARY DAWNED BRIGHT AND warm. Just as spring renews the earth, I felt a renewed surge of optimism. They were treating Rob's cancer aggressively, which meant he was very sick, but he was home with the family and we'd put together some semblance of a "new normal" for ourselves.

We had our first physical therapy training session since returning home and I was happy to hear that all of Rob's muscles were working, we just needed to strengthen them. The doctors all agreed that Rob needed to put on more weight and drink more fluids. To me, that felt like an easy answer. He was weak but all I had to do was feed him and hydrate him, and eventually, he'd get better.

On February 2, Rob graduated from radiation for the time being and, I hoped, forever. Doctor Hoffelt explained to us what Rob's body was going through and how the radiation had affected him. The treatment only took two weeks, and I asked Doctor Hoffelt why that was, since I knew of other patients who'd received treatment for eight weeks.

Rob graduating from radiation

"With other cancers, you do radiation little by little at every visit until it kills the cancer," Doctor Hoffelt explained. "But with melanoma, you have to do as much radiation as the person can handle as quickly as possible without killing them."

He added that, with Rob's young age and good health, he attacked the cancer as aggressively as he could. It reassured Rob, who wasn't used to feeling sick. Now he understood that he'd felt like death the last few weeks because he'd been brought so close to it.

Rob told me he could see a light at the end of the tunnel. The worst was now behind us; radiation was over and Rob was on the mend. He even felt well enough to write on our family blog on February 3:

> *Looks like you get to hear from me tonight, so hopefully that's a good thing. Got ready to go to church (pain), and our air conditioning (at the church building) broke and church was canceled. I get all ready and no church. Things are getting better. My legs are*

starting to hurt which we hope is an indication of some of the feeling coming back. Throat is still sore and it's hard to eat. Day by day, right?

Love,

Rob

In a talk given by Dennis E. Simmons, he said, "Faith is believing that although we do not understand all things, He (Christ) does. Faith is knowing that, although our power is limited, His is not. Faith in Jesus Christ consists of complete reliance in Him. . . . We must understand that great challenges make great men."[6]

I'd gotten good at recognizing all the miracles and blessings in my life, great and small. Little things seemed to happen every day. Nice weather appeared whenever I needed to get Rob in or out of the car. It still rained—this was Portland, after all—but the skies always cleared up right when I needed them to.

We had a steady stream of sweet visitors. People from Rob's work came by to assure him that the company was behind him. Friends from his softball team stopped in to give us a donation. Friends and family were still volunteering to stay with us and help take care of the family.

As February wore on, Rob continued to improve. He was still weak and struggling with his physical therapy, but without the radiation

Rob holding John and Luke. They loved sitting in the wheel chair with their dada

treatments, he had more energy and I could see that he was getting better and stronger every day. Even friends from our congregation commented to me that Rob looked better, noting that he had color in his face and was able to keep his eyes open for the whole visit.

Rob wrote on the blog, February 7:

> *Howdy all. I thought I'd give Patti a break tonight. Not so much you guys, but she deserves one. Lying on your back and typing with one hand is not so easy. Lots happened today. . . . No Mitt! McCain, really!? Sorry!*
>
> *Oh, we can talk sick stuff now, I guess. I had a good day. I was able to bathe, which is a pain. I shaved, which is big. I did not do a great job, but the beard is gone. Pretty sure we are putting on weight, despite how much I hate to eat. Patti and Caren snuck protein into my Rice Krispies this morning. Haha.*
>
> *A new family is coming in [to stay with us]; which*

1997 Epperson Cruise for Granna and Shramps 50th wedding anniversary. Me, Rob, Granna and Shramps

Wherefore Didst Thou Doubt?

Rob, his dad and Shramps doing one of their most favorite hobbies, golfing

> we love. This is kind of a drastic way to get people to
> visit us, but we get to see Betsy Cannon, Liza Mitchell,
> Granna and Schramps, my dad and brothers, and I
> know many more. Thank you, thank you.
> I love you all.
> Robbie

Spring is a beautiful season, but there are still rainstorms and we had a small one on February 8, when I took Rob to physical therapy. I was trying to hide my frustration, but I felt like they weren't doing enough to help Rob walk again. I watched the moves they did with him and wondered why I'd carted him all the way over to the hospital when I could've done the exact same things at home, myself.

Then, at the end of the appointment, they told us they wanted to cut down his visits from three times a week to twice a week.

Shramps, Robbie, and Rob

"His arms and trunk—the core of his body—are too weak," the doctor said. "Physical therapy isn't going to be of much help until he builds up more strength."

I wanted to ask them if they were throwing in the towel, if this was their way of letting me know they didn't think Rob would ever walk again. The therapist could see I was getting upset, so he sat us down and explained in more detail what was happening with Rob's body and why this was the best course of action for him.

"Once his strength gets better, we can go back to three days a week," he said.

I realized we'd been too focused on the progress he was making with his legs and we didn't give enough attention to his arms and core. I swallowed back my disappointment and resolved to do better at home. We were going to work harder, I told myself, whether Rob wanted to or not!

There were more tears two days later, when we sent home some much beloved family members. Granna, Schramps, Aunt Liza, and Aunt Caren all flew home in the morning. Ellie was especially devastated about Aunt Caren because they'd formed a unique bond in their time together. For the first time since December 15, we were alone as a family.

Aunt Caren reading to Ellie

But the break was short-lived because that same night, Rob's Aunt Betsy and Uncle Craig flew in. Our family alone time lasted only twelve hours. I once again marveled at how blessed we were to be part of such a close-knit family, and at how willing everyone around us was to serve us in whatever way we needed.

Aunt Betsy was a special blessing for me. Her son, John, had suffered with and survived cancer when he was 16 years old. Now 21, he was serving a church mission in Baltimore. She was a point of light and hope. In a very unique and real way, she understood what I was going through as a caregiver. And not only that, but she'd done it and her son survived.

Looking back now, it may be hard to remember how different the world was in 2008. Facebook wasn't a household name yet. Google was barely a word I'd heard of and smart phones were brand new. Doing a quick internet search to find information about something was still an

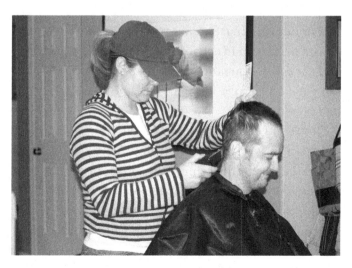

Rob's hair was falling out everywhere, so it was finally time to shave his head. Brandie was so sweet to come over and do it for us.

Rob with his new haircut

untested science, at least in my life. When it came to my varied and limitless questions about cancer, chemo and the recovery process, I felt virtually helpless.

When we were sent home from the doctors, they warned me to watch Rob for signs of any unusual symptoms. What I wanted to scream out was, "What are *usual* symptoms?" I had no idea what was normal for a cancer patient. I had no idea what was abnormal either. I watched Rob like a hawk and every cough, sore throat, or ache terrified me.

With Betsy's arrival came a fountain of knowledge and understanding. She was truly the answer to prayer. Before her, I couldn't claim to know another soul who'd had cancer or gone through radiation. I knew nothing but what I'd learned in the month and a half since Rob had gotten sick.

"Rob's fingertips are numb," I told her one day, in a near panic. "What does that mean?"

"I remember John losing feeling in his fingertips," she said casually. She let out a small laugh. "I had to button his shirts for him."

"Rob's throat is hurting so much he won't eat," I said later, worry creasing my brow.

"I remember John's throat hurting like that," she said, patting my arm.

"Rob's steroids were reduced," I told her the next day, unsure. "I feel like we're missing something because he's still weak."

Betsy sighed and nodded. "It took John a long time to get over them reducing his steroids. He was so weak!"

I almost collapsed into tears, I was so relieved. Such simple assurances meant the world to me. Yes, this was scary but it was typical and maybe, in five years, I'd be comforting someone else who has a loved one with cancer, assuring them as easily as Betsy assured me.

The burden of a cancer caregiver is a unique one, and something I was very naïve about at first. Cancer is a hard and horrible disease. When you're a caregiver, you're healthy but you have to help someone who is completely dependent on you, someone who is suffering immensely. Someone who is scared, someone who needs your comfort and confidence in them.

As the caregiver, you need to be all things: a medical advocate, a support system, an insurance expert, a nurse, a partner, and a CEO who takes care of all the other daily tasks that the cancer patient can't do anymore, on top of whatever else you were responsible for in your normal life.

It was exhausting, but I couldn't complain because I knew my suffering was nothing compared to Rob's. I was still human. I still felt angry and frustrated, grumpy and tired. But now, instead of letting it out or taking a much-needed break, I stuffed it all in and felt guilty at my own imperfectness. I wasn't dying, so whatever my complaints were, however tired I was, it was nothing compared to what Rob was dealing with, I told myself.

I kept a regular blog for our friends and family and in it, I made sure my tone was positive and optimistic. But the reality was Rob was very sick and I was very scared.

I was literally running myself to my absolute limits on a daily basis. How could I not? The bills still needed to be paid, the kids still needed to be cared for, and my husband was reduced to a newborn, requiring all the attention and care that any other helpless being does. There was no time to worry about myself, if I was eating enough or sleeping enough.

Betsy breathed new life into me. She let me talk to her about my own struggles. She helped me realize that a lot of Rob's symptoms and pain were totally normal. And she gave me hope that we could make it through this trial, just like she did five years earlier.

Valentine's Day was approaching fast but I knew our usual tradition of celebrating as a family wasn't likely to

Valentine's Day 2006

Valentine's Day 2007

happen this year. In the past, the boys would dress in their Sunday best, buy flowers for Ellie and me, and then we'd all go out to dinner together. It was a fun opportunity to train my sons on how to behave like gentlemen.

Because we couldn't go out as a family, Rob and I decided to arrange a visit to the Portland temple instead. It was such a blessing that we both had current temple recommends. We'd always made that a priority—renewing them at least a month before they expired, so we'd never be in a position where we couldn't go. I know Rob could've attained one if it had come to that, but everything drained his limited energy. It was nice to have one less thing to worry about.

We gathered a group of close friends and got a sitter for the kids. Years earlier, our church leaders encouraged us to buy our own temple clothes as an additional measure of being prepared for temple service. I'd heeded

Valentine's Day 2008: Lauren, me, Rob, Kerry and Shane Bowman

this advice then and it was a relief on Valentine's Day because we were able to get Rob dressed in his white suit at home after realizing it would be near impossible to get him ready at the temple, where men and women dress in separate locker rooms.

It made me realize how important it is to continually keep yourself worthy and ready. When the need arises, will you be ready? It had been less than two months since Rob first got sick. The cancer came on so fast, we had no time to prepare for it. But that's usually how it is with life's greatest trials—they come quickly. If you aren't ready beforehand, there's no time to get ready during the trial.

The Celestial Room, an especially important place of reverence in our temples, was beautiful and peaceful that day. We were able to move Rob from his wheelchair onto one of the couches so that he could sit and ponder. The spirit of the Lord was powerful as we sat side by side in this room full of symbols of our eternal promises to each other. Being there on Valentine's Day made it bittersweet.

Valentine's Day 2008: Rob and I at the temple

Wherefore Didst Thou Doubt?

Valentine's Day 2008: Jake, me and Ellie at Big Al's

Our earthly future was uncertain at this point, but I had confidence that our eternal relationship would continue on past this trial.

Instead of going out as a whole family, I took the older three kids to dinner. We tried to escape the reality of our lives, even if it was just for one hour. While we waited for our food, the kids realized they finally had their mom all to themselves for the first time in awhile. No one else was around. They knew I never lied to them (which can be a bad thing sometimes), and that I would answer the one question no one else would dare answer for them: Is Daddy going to die? As three sets of eyes stared at me, I told them exactly what I felt.

"NO, Daddy isn't going to die!" I said it firmly, leaving no room for doubt. I felt the truth of my words with all of my body; there was no way he would ever leave us. He couldn't and he wouldn't *ever* leave us. I reassured them that all would be fine. I knew it. Because I believed in miracles and this was going to be a miracle!

I wrote on our family blog the next day:

Yesterday I found myself unable to buy Valentine's stuff for the kids. I can't explain it, but I just didn't have the heart for it. In the past, we spent Valentine's Day as a family. I knew we wouldn't be having our Valentine tradition tonight. Thank goodness so many people listened to the spirit and showered our family with Valentine love today!! We got flowers, cards, gift packages, so many wonderful things, my kids didn't even notice that mom was a little sad. I took the kids to Big Al's for arcade and bowling, and let them get whatever they wanted for dinner. Jake had a pound of steamed clams. They all got special drinks and didn't even have to share. I then let them play all the video games they liked, especially the ones we usually don't let them play. We all had a blast.

On the way home, I was a little sad that Rob couldn't be there with us. Robbie asked me what was wrong and I said, "Aren't you sad that Dad couldn't come?" Robbie and Jake both said yes, but if Dad wasn't sick, the twins wouldn't have come and we wouldn't have gone to Big Al's at all.

My little boys were teaching me a valuable lesson. They were looking at the positive of the situation. They weren't saying it in a snotty way, but were sincere with their answer. I will forever be grateful for that moment. My boys trying to comfort me and helping me understand that there are many blessings I'm not seeing. They are such sweet, strong boys who are taking on more than any boy their age should.

I hope everyone felt loved today. Thank you once again, for everyone who reached out to us today. For

Wherefore Didst Thou Doubt?

*listening and answering a mother's simple prayer so
her children could have a loving day!*

Love,

Patti

There's no light without dark, and good days are often followed by bad ones. The day after Valentine's Day, we were told by Rob's physical therapists that he was too weak to continue the sessions. He simply wasn't progressing at all. There was no way to continue treating him.

We'd also just been told that Rob couldn't receive any more chemo treatments until his platelets stabilized. I teased him that he must be Edward from the Twilight books because he was in such desperate need of blood. But the truth was, I'd become a bit frustrated at Rob's lack of improvement.

When I was at the temple the day before, I prayed fervently for the ability to understand God's will for us. I was studying my lesson for church (I was still the Gospel Doctrine teacher), and I was drawn to the section on agency.

Agency is such an integral part of our lives. Being able to choose right over wrong, making choices for ourselves—this is at the core of our earthly journey. I knew that God won't do for you what you can do for yourself. He also won't make choices for you. You must choose for yourself. I was irritated with Rob because I felt like he wasn't choosing to get better. I knew he felt horrible. I knew it hurt to eat. But he still needed to! Prayer alone couldn't make him gain weight. Prayer alone couldn't make him stronger. I did everything I could: I made the food, I helped with exercises at home, I made the doctor's appointments, picked up the medicine and took him where he needed to go. But I couldn't force him to eat. I couldn't force him to push his body forward.

"It's hard," I told him as I tried to explain my thought process. "I feel like you're not fighting for this as hard as you need to. I am taking on all the responsibilities and all this stress; I'm balancing all these different things in our lives. All I need you to do is eat. Please just eat."

Rob admitted that he was mad at me for all my pushing, but that he also knew I was right. Eating hurt but he had to do it. After that, he ate everything I put in front of him for the rest of the day. The next morning, he got up, did all his exercises and even showered—all before noon!

I'd felt awful for being hard on him earlier but to see him trying again made it all seem worth it. I was a bit worried though, because it was time for Aunt Betsy and Uncle Craig to return home. I didn't know what I would do without Betsy and her constant support and wisdom. I consoled myself that my sisters, Janet and Kathy, would be arriving soon.

Before they left, Uncle Craig gave Rob a blessing. It was truly beautiful. Craig talked about how Rob had touched many lives for the better and how our Heavenly Father was mindful of him and watching over him. He added that our Savior knew the pain and suffering Rob was enduring and They were by his side, so he could turn to them in this time of need.

I knew Rob was already aware of this, but sometimes you need to hear it again.

The rest of the week, Rob continued to eat well. It might've helped that my sisters were just as focused as I was on getting Rob to eat. I wondered if he was shoveling the food into his mouth because it was the only way to keep us quiet. But he had more energy, seemed more alert, and was sleeping less during the daytime. Rob told me he was determined to prove his physical therapist wrong and work even harder on his exercises.

That Sunday, Rob was released from his church calling, which meant he was without a calling for the first time in years. After Uncle Craig's blessing though, I felt sure that Rob was still serving the Lord—more now than he had before, just by sharing his testimony and being such a great example to everyone we met on this journey.

In light of all Rob's recent improvements, I felt sure that the worst was now behind us. I remembered the words Uncle Craig spoke in his blessing: how the Savior was mindful of Rob. What a great comfort and blessing to know the power of heaven was a prayer away. With the Lord on our side, what did we have to fear?

CHAPTER 5

February 2008

Let us cheerfully do all things that lie in our power; and then may we stand still, with the utmost assurance, to see the salvation of God, and for his arm to be revealed.

Doctrine and Covenants 123:17

On February 20, we were back in the hospital.

The day before had been rough. Rob's brother was in town so we'd all taken him out, thinking a visit to Target might be fun. But while there, Rob got confused and disoriented. He said he'd spoken with someone about finding a folder and insisted that he needed to stand in the aisle and wait for this person's return.

"Rob, we've been with you the whole time," I tried to explain. "You didn't talk to anyone about a folder. We don't even need folders."

We finally got him home, but it was clear he was still confused. I tried not to let his behavior worry me too much, but I couldn't help feeling scared. I never knew what issues were caused by the cancer, what was caused by the radiation, or what was caused by the medication. I remembered him acting in a similar manner before they put the shunt in his brain. I hoped it was only that the doctors needed to check on it and adjust it, then Rob would be back to normal. Or at least, back to our new normal.

We invited our friends, Brother Anderson and Brother Denfeld, over to give Rob and me blessings (in our religion, we refer to other adult members as "Brother" or "Sister" before their last name to show that we are all one family under God). When Brother Anderson told Rob, in his blessing, that Heavenly Father was very aware of his situation and was with him, I felt the spirit burn in my chest—testifying to the truth of these words. When it was my turn, I was told that I needed to be an advocate for Rob and that I would be given the strength I needed to help him, serve my children, and continue in my calling as Gospel Doctrine teacher.

I felt like all the stress and worry, all the burdens piled on my shoulders, were lifted off. It amazed me. I had all the same troubles and responsibilities I'd had before the blessing. But now I felt stronger, more hopeful. And most of all, I felt like I wasn't doing this alone.

When we went to the hospital on February 20, the doctors adjusted Rob's shunt, which eased his confusion. The shunt controlled the flow of spinal fluid around his brain and could be adjusted by putting a magnet near the back of his head to move it as needed. The doctors also gave him an MRI to see if there were any new issues. They reminded me that it would be about a month before we'd be able to see how well Rob's radiation treatments had worked.

Then we went to the infusion center to give Rob an infusion of new blood. They always put us in a private room by ourselves. It took about an hour for the treat-

Some of the players from our co-ed soccer team

ment to run its course. I often curled up on the bed next to him. This was before the days of easy wifi and smart phones, so we'd lay there and talk or flip through the TV channels until it was time to go.

While lying beside him on this day, I let my mind wander back to a year ago, when Rob was still healthy.

We were playing on our co-ed soccer team. During one of our games, as I raced across the field to assist with a goal, I got tangled up with a woman on the opposing team and we both hit the ground hard. Her husband came running over to us, crying foul and yelling at me for hurting his wife. The man was red with anger and got close enough to me that I was worried he would hit me. Rob came flying out from the player's box, ready to defend me. He was held back by a mutual friend, but he was so fierce and focused on getting to me he ended up with bruises on his arms from the force required to hold him back.

After the game, our friends joked that he looked like Edward from the Twilight movie, ready to go full vampire in defense of the woman he loved.

Wherefore Didst Thou Doubt?

"If I'd known you guys were going to compare me to Edward, I would've sat back and let that guy go after her," Rob grumbled. Such was his dislike of Edward and the whole Twilight saga.

But Edward he was, in a way. Rob needed blood infusions regularly and nothing perked him up like a transfusion treatment.

Every time we visited, the doctors would ask me if I wanted to check Rob in and have him stay at the hospital. I understood why they asked. Rob was down to 144 pounds and he was very sick. Everything he needed was in that building. My life would be easier if I didn't have to drag him back and forth. But I felt very strongly that Rob needed to be at home; he needed to be with the kids. In a way, I worried that checking him in meant we were giving up on him. It was hard having a sick husband in the house, but it was miles better than not having him there at all. So a lot of my focus was on that: keeping Rob home. This mean that sometimes I downplayed our struggles.

"Yes, it's hard to get him in and out of the wheelchair, but there's always someone nearby to help," I would tell the nurse with a laugh.

"I know he was disoriented at Target, but once they adjusted the shunt, he was totally fine," I assured Dr. Liss.

"He's weak and not eating, but a quick IV and some more pain medication is all we need," I said to the doctor on call, hoping he didn't see that under my frozen smile, I was beginning to crack.

To me, this is what it meant to be Rob's advocate. He needed to be at home with his family, so I did everything I could to make that happen. And when I came up short, I got him what he needed from the doctors and nothing more.

I'd feel nervous and exposed, standing under the fluorescent lights above the check in counter as I tried to assure the nurses that this was a quick visit and not a long stay. I'd feel relieved when we were done and I was able to wheel him back out to the car.

But at 2 a.m. on February 22, I found myself sitting in an unfamiliar emergency room at a hospital a half hour away from home, scared that my luck had run out.

Rob's pain medications had stopped working that day, and he was miserable. Earlier in the evening, I'd driven him to our regular ER. But we'd been waiting for two hours in a full waiting room before I gave up and brought him back home.

A friend who was visiting suggested we call an ambulance. When an ambulance brings a patient into the ER, that patient is rushed to the head of the queue. Considering we'd been at the ER for hours with no movement, this seemed like the only way to get Rob some relief, so I took the advice.

But when the ambulance came, they discovered that every nearby hospital was full and the nearest one that could take us was a 30 minute drive away. This hospital didn't have any connection to our usual one which meant they didn't have access to any of Rob's records. I had to explain everything related to Rob's situation: his cancer, the radiation, the treatment plans, the shunt in his brain, the different medications he'd been on and was now on. I almost felt ready to test for a medical degree, I'd become so familiar with medical terminology.

I wrote on our family blog later:

> *I realized earlier today that we have just started this battle. When you really think about it, Rob has only done radiation once, on two parts of his body. He had chemo meds during radiation, but a small amount. He was supposed to continue his chemo after radiation, but he had these rashes, so we decided to wait. So technically, he hasn't even been through a complete session of chemo. We do have an appointment with Doctor Urba next Wednesday. He has been following our treatment so far and it will be nice to talk to him again. So we are in the ER because Rob started having pains in his left side. They were sharp pains and new ones. I gave him some morphine and it helped some; but he was still restless and in pain. We called an ambulance to pick him up and the closest hospital taking patients was in Portland by Mall 205 (at least two hospitals away from our house). They are doing another scan of his head and also his belly. I am not sure if we will find anything out. Who knows, at this point nothing surprises me.*

I've always been someone who is determined to find the bright side in any situation and the optimist in me didn't fail me this night, even though I was tired and frustrated. In the end, it was a good thing we ended up at a strange hospital because they decided not to check him in since they didn't have any of his records and he was used to working with a different staff. This meant we weren't at risk of Rob being forced to stay in the hospital indefinitely. Had we waited for our turn at our regular ER, that may not have been the case. Once we got to the hospital, and after they completed the CT scans, Rob was finally able to fall asleep.

We got home at seven a.m., bleary-eyed and ready to climb into my bed just as the kids were bouncing out of theirs. My sisters, Janet and Kathy, were staying with us so Rob and I were able to sleep until one that afternoon.

When we woke up, the afternoon sunlight streaming in and the house peaceful, Rob turned to me. His eyes were alert but sad.

"Do you want take backs?" he asked.

"What?" I asked, rubbing the sleep from my eyes.

He lay still, his body weak and paralyzed. He blinked back tears and repeated the question. "Do you want take backs? Do you want to switch me out for someone else?"

I pulled myself up on my elbows. "Never," I said, pouring all the love I had for him into that one word. I laughed to cover up my desire to cry. The question—and him feeling the need to ask it—broke my heart. But he sounded like his old self, and it also renewed my hope of a full recovery. "I can't love you any more than I do right now," I whispered, leaning over to kiss him.

Rob's question and my firm reply seemed to rejuvenate him. The next few days, he ate well, slept well, and had many moments of alertness and clarity. The arrival of his cousin, Jackson, perked him up as well. My sisters had been visiting for a week and I think Rob was happy to get a little more testosterone around.

Rob was on a lot of pain medication, which meant he spent a lot of time sleeping, but he did his best to visit

Wherefore Didst Thou Doubt?

Me and my sisters: Kathy and Janet

June 9, 1995 our wedding day

Die hard BYU fans!

Our Christmas card 2004 (picture taken at Kathy's wedding)

Rob and I on our first anniversary

with Jackson. I felt bad because whenever Rob had visitors, they spent most of the time with me since Rob slept constantly.

"Today has been a good day," Rob told me the evening of February 23, as I got him ready for bed. "Why have the last two days been so good?"

I thought back on the last few days. The ER visit earlier in the week had been scary, but Jackson's visit had brought a lot of laughter and joy into our home. And earlier, we'd been blessed by a longtime family friend, Matt Elerding. We'd met because our sons played baseball together and Matt was fascinated by our family. He grew up Catholic but wasn't religious. He was a successful businessman in the mortgage industry and owned a beautiful, huge house. He couldn't believe we didn't drink or smoke, and we had all these kids running around all the time. Our life looked completely different from his, and from what he imagined a happy life would look like. But happy we

Jackson and Rob having to endure the Oscars with me and my sisters

Wherefore Didst Thou Doubt?

Matt (Rob Epperson games) and Luke

were. And he adored Rob. He thought Rob was the most amazing person ever.

When Rob got sick, it floored a lot of people, but Matt especially struggled with it. "What kind of God would do that to such a wonderful family man?" he asked me once.

Every year, Matt would hold the "Man Games". They did silly things like swim across an unheated pool to prove how "manly" they were. This year, the games were held on February 24, and though Rob couldn't participate, we were invited to come enjoy the festivities.

When we got there toward the end of the event, we were surprised to find out that Matt was holding this year's games in Rob's honor, even renaming them the "Rob Epperson Games". He'd gathered 20 of his friends, men we barely knew or had never met before, and had gotten them all to donate money to help us pay our medical bills. I could see the love Matt had for Rob and I noticed how much Matt's friends cared for Rob, despite not really knowing him. I wondered if I could be that generous or loving to people I'd never even met. I knew many people out there who we hadn't personally met were reading our family blog and praying for us. It was such a lesson for me that most people are truly *good*.

At the end of the night, Rob was exhausted and a couple of the men, including Matt, helped me put him in the car and load up the wheelchair. Watching them help my frail husband really showed me how much the disease had ravaged him. At the Man Games last year, he was the same size as any of them. Now, he looked like a child in their arms. And, try as they might, they couldn't hide their tears. They couldn't hide how affected they were by Rob's condition. Seeing their reaction shook me.

When we got home and I pulled into the driveway, I stopped the car and turned to my husband.

"Rob, are you dying?" I asked him, my voice catching on the last word.

"No, I'm not." He stared back, unflinching.

"Okay," I said, letting out a relieved laugh. That's all I needed. Rob was my best friend and I trusted him completely. If he said he wasn't going anywhere, I'd believe him, despite the evidence of my eyes.

That night, I wrote on our family blog:

> *Tonight I was again thinking of the story of Abraham and Isaac. Instead of thinking of the walk up the mountain, I was thinking of the walk down the mountain. How happy they must have been, knowing they had been faithful in being obedient to God's commandment and also that Isaac was still alive! I*

wonder if they chatted excitedly (probably not, because they weren't girls) or if they walked down in silence pondering what had just happened. We will have that walk down the mountain. I don't know when or how, but I trust in the Lord with all my heart!

Love,
Patti

The next week and a half, Rob continued to improve. He put more weight on, he was moving his toes, his blood levels were up, and we were able to lower his morphine levels. It was as if when he told me he wasn't going to die, he set out to prove it.

The hope and excitement was spilling out of me when I updated our family blog on February 25:

We have even better news today! We had Rob's doctor's appointment this afternoon and first off, he gained three pounds in five days! We can thank my sisters for feeding him such wonderful food (homemade chicken noodle soup, seafood fettuccine and salmon). Also, when they did his blood work, his numbers were wonderful. He didn't need any blood or platelets. This is great because we want his platelet levels to come up so he can start his oral chemo again. And if his levels didn't come up, we would need to put another shunt in his head for the chemo instead of the chemo pills.

We are so happy with the doctor visit today. This was honestly the first time we didn't have to get blood or an IV. Doctor Liss looked at Rob moving his feet and said he is doing it more from his hip flexors than the foot muscles. It is still great news, because he couldn't do that before and now he can.

Again, I want to thank everyone who is praying for us! We received a Prayer Shawl from my brother-in-law's mother, Syl Walton. The shawl is knitted for anyone who is ill or going through a challenging time in their life. Syl's friend gave this to her for Rob. I am so humbled by the many people who are concerned for us and want to help however they can. It is a beautiful shawl and keeps him very warm. We also got a wonderful framed scripture from our Aunt Caren's friend, Chris Rasche. It's from Peter 1:16: "Be ye holy for I am holy."

I know we are strong because of everyone praying and helping us. Let's pray for even better days to come!

Love,
Patti

Family sitting around, watching BYU volleyball

"I'm on cloud nine," I told my sister Janet two days later. "His legs are moving more. I know anyone else probably couldn't tell a difference, but I can."

Nights were still rough because Rob was like a newborn. He'd often wake me up and ask me to move or adjust him so he could get more comfortable. You don't realize how much you move during the night until you need someone to do the moving for you. But even though it made it hard to get a good night's sleep when he woke me up to rub his legs at one a.m., I didn't mind too much because I was excited he could feel his legs enough to be bothered by them.

We had an appointment with Doctor Urba on February 28. I asked friends and family to pray for the doctor, that he might be enlightened as to what the best treatment options would be for Rob. I had a lot of faith in Doctor Urba. I felt certain he was going to solve this for us. Why else would the Lord have placed an expert in Rob's specific type of cancer so nearby?

CHAPTER 6

MARCH 2008

If any of you lack wisdom, let him ask of God, that giveth to all men liberally, and upbraideth not; and it shall be given him. But let him ask in faith, nothing wavering.

JAMES 1:5–6

NEEDED A MIRACLE AND I knew how to get one. If I had enough faith, a miracle would happen. God is a God of miracles and this miracle was going to stand as a testimony for many that God truly answers prayers. I had a strong testimony of the power of fasting and it just so happened that an important doctor's appointment for Rob was right before fast Sunday. To me, that was a sign.

I'd realized I would need more help after meeting with Doctor Urba the week before. I'd gone with my stepmother, Sheri, because I was at a point where I could no longer lift or move Rob on my own. Even though he'd lost a lot of weight, I didn't have the strength to get him in and out of the car by myself.

Rob was completely passed out, due to his pain medication. A nurse had to help us put him on the examination table. He slept through his entire appointment and Doctor

Urba seemed concerned by Rob's general appearance and sluggishness. I assured him it was only because of the morphine.

The doctor sat down in a chair next to Rob's sleeping frame and studied him for a few silent minutes. "He's still on morphine?" Doctor Urba asked.

I nodded.

"Does he always sleep like this when he's on it?"

Believe in Miracles poster for Rob

"We'd taken him off it for awhile because he'd get confused and sleep nonstop," I said. "But this morning he was in pain, so we gave him some."

"And when he takes it, he's always like this?" Doctor Urba asked.

"No, no," I said in a rush. "He's been doing great! Really."

Sheri and I

Doctor Urba kept his face passive but that spoke as much as any other expression could have and I felt my stomach clench. *Don't give up on Rob,* I silently pleaded. *Don't give up on us.*

"We're basically dealing with two different types of cancer because of the locations," Doctor Urba said, moving on to the business at hand—much to my relief. "The first is the melanoma in his central nervous system—his brain and spine. I've looked over the scans we took of Rob last week and it seems the radiation treatment worked at containing the cancer and even shrinking it some."

I sucked in a breath and clasped my hands together, my face lighting up in a hopeful smile. But Doctor Urba held up a hand as if to stop me from getting too excited.

"Then we have the melanoma in the rest of his body," Doctor Urba said. "We'll need to get Rob a full body scan to see if the cancer has increased. That could be what's causing his weakness and body pain. And the way he's reacting to the morphine makes me concerned that the cancer may have spread to his liver."

I nodded my understanding, but honestly, I hadn't heard much past when he said it looked like the cancer had shrunk. "So when can we start chemo again?" I asked.

"The numbers from his blood test are way too low," Doctor Urba said, explaining what the minimum level should be and how Rob's numbers weren't there.

"Okay, what can we do to get those levels up?" I asked. "Can we start the chemo as we work toward that?" "I really don't—" Doctor Urba paused, looking at Rob, still asleep on the examination table. "He's a very, very sick boy," Doctor Urba said, his voice soft.

"I have faith that Rob will come through," I said, holding a hand to my heart as tears welled up in my eyes. I could feel the spirit burning in my chest and I tried to funnel this power into my words. "I know it won't be some magical miracle, but I believe in you, Doctor Urba. I know, without a doubt that you're going to be the Lord's instrument in bringing about the answers to my prayers."

Doctor Urba's eyes scanned the room. He looked from me to Rob, then to Sheri, to the nurse standing silently by the door, and back to me. Sometime during my speech, the nurse had begun to cry and I could see Sheri wiping at her cheeks, as well.

No one spoke for several minutes as Doctor Urba seemed to process what I'd said and what that meant for him. Finally he sighed, his shoulders slumping slightly. "Bring Rob back on Monday," he said, rubbing the bridge of his nose. "If his numbers are up, we can start more chemo."

"Yes," I said, breathing out the word like a victory chant. "Yes. Thank you, Doctor Urba!"

Doctor Urba was doing his best, as a medical professional, to bring Rob through this. I decided I needed to do my part to bring the power of Heaven in to help him.

On the drive home, Sheri and I discussed the visit and I was surprised to find her notes and general impression of what Doctor Urba had said were very different from mine. She felt much less hopeful than I did and thought the doctor was only agreeing to reconsider chemo to appease me in that moment.

I wrote on our family blog on March 1:

> *I hope I'm able to explain what is ahead for us for everyone to understand. And I hope that I understood what the doctors all said to us. I've already noticed that two people at the same appointment can hear two different things. Sheri came to Doctor Urba's with me and as we compared notes, we came out with different understandings, so my impressions may be wrong, but all I can tell everyone is what I think I understand.*

We're going about this day by day. I can't plan anything even a couple days in advance because I have no idea how Rob will be feeling. First, let me give everyone a better idea of how Rob is doing. Rob can only sit up in bed for short periods of time, maybe 15 minutes. He'd rather be lying down in bed. We tried to move him out to the couch, but it's not comfortable for him and he wanted to get back into bed.

Every time we get him into or out of his wheelchair, we have to physically lift him (typically two people) into his chair or bed. He can't sit up in bed by himself; someone has to pull him to a sitting position.

Lately, he hasn't been wanting to sit in his wheelchair for longer than 20 minutes—it hurts too much. He's had a hard time carrying on conversations. He gets confused easily and tired mentally. Even watching the Jazz play, he has a hard time following the game. It's a good day if he stays awake for longer than an hour. He has been declining with each week. While there are many positive steps in the past week, he is very sick.

Now to what the doctor said. We don't know what is going to be happening next week. Rob will have his body scan on Monday. Once the results come back, then the doctors will decide what steps we'll be taking. I have no idea when or what type of chemo Rob will be having. If the cancer has been growing throughout his body aggressively, he will have chemo for the body cancer and a separate chemo for his cancer in the central nervous system.

But again, we won't know this till the scan comes back. Everything takes time. I don't know when they'll start chemo again, nor do I know how much or where. I'm trying to keep everyone up to date, but I know things get lost in translation. Just like Sheri and I heard two different things at the doctors, I know stories get confused as they are retold.

I hope this has been somewhat insightful to many as to what it's like here. I was upset at first that Rob couldn't get his scan until Monday, but then it dawned on me that Fast Sunday is this Sunday. What a perfect opportunity we all have to fast for Rob.

I don't know yet what the Lord's will is, but my first instinct would be to fast that the cancer in his body is not spreading aggressively. We already know he has cancer all over his body, but that it hasn't spread since his last scan.

For those who have never fasted before, you go without food or drink for two meals. You start and end with a prayer. Anyone can do this, if it's medically okay! Thank you all for your support and love.

Love,
Patti

During this time, members of our church congregation circled around my family and kept us afloat. We were lucky because there were lots of police officers and men with unusual work hours so they could come at different times during the day, depending on when they were needed. I hadn't been taking care of myself and had no hope of lifting Rob and helping him with basic tasks like taking a shower without help.

"It's amazing how many men are coming to help out," Sheri said one morning as some members of our church helped Rob into his wheelchair so he could join us for breakfast.

I nodded my agreement. We were lucky. We lived in a relatively young congregation and most of the families were around our age. At least once a day, a male member came over to help us. They'd help Rob to the car or back into the house, they'd carry him up or down the stairs, they helped him take showers or go through his physical therapy exercises. And they did it with such an eagerness to help, as if they were grateful for the opportunity to be there.

"It can't be easy for them seeing Rob this sick," I said to Sheri. "I'm in awe of them. All we have to do is call and someone will be right over to help."

When I put the word out that I wanted to do a fast for Rob that Sunday, March 2, many from our church joined us, along with friends and family—even those who didn't share our faith. To fast in our religion means you begin with a prayer, fast for two meals, and then close with a prayer before the next meal. Sometimes I'd cheat when fasting. I'd have a big dinner Saturday evening, then go to church the next morning and have an early dinner. But during this time, our church met from 3 p.m. to 6 p.m., which meant no cheating. It would be a true, 24-hour fast by the time I got home and was able to eat again.

There was much regarding Rob that weighed on my mind, but I decided to focus my prayers through the fast on the hope that the medicine would work and that the doctors would find a way to treat his cancer. I also prayed simply that everything would work out. I was still very optimistic at this point.

I also prayed to know what was going to happen. I was an organizer, a planner. I liked taking a pen to my calendar and getting my life mapped out. But with Rob sick, there were no absolutes and I couldn't make plans for even a day ahead of time. Saturday, as I began my fast, I sat outside to watch the sunset with Sheri. It was a beautiful clear day, but the early spring weather was forcing my mind forward. I couldn't help wondering what our future was going to look like.

In the safety and comfort of her company, I let myself unload some of my stress.

"How am I going to do this?" I asked her helplessly. "Rob's brother, Jimmy, is getting married in April. It's in Utah." I paused to look at Sheri and let that sink in. "I can't even get Rob to the hospital without help. How can I get him to Utah? How can I push a wheelchair and a double stroller?"

Sheri's eyes were full of a deep sadness as she looked at me. She wrapped an arm around my shoulders and let me cry as I wailed about the logistics of traveling with a cancer-ridden husband.

"I'm tired," I admitted. "I'm so exhausted."

"Of course you are," Sheri murmured, rubbing my arm. "Just let it out."

So I did. I sat beside her and cried until the sun had slunk away and all my tears were gone.

I woke up Sunday to find my twins were sick with a cold. I intended to fast no matter what, but I was a little worried about going to church. With Rob's deteriorating condition, there was no way I could expect Sheri to care for him *and* my sick twins. But as I was discussing options with Sheri, my phone rang. Sandy Ririe, my Institute teacher, had called.

As soon as I said, "Hello?" she said matter-of-factly, "How can I help you?"

I breathed out a grateful sigh as I asked her to come help Sheri take care of the family. Her delight at actually being needed was clear, even through the phone, and she rushed over.

During church, I repeated my silent prayers for Rob. *Help the medicine work. Help the doctors know how to heal him. Help me know what's going to happen.* Like a mantra, my pleading played through my mind on repeat.

As I sat in Sacrament meeting, my children lined up beside me on the pew, the fact that Rob was missing was more palpable than usual. My stomach twisted with hunger and my heart ached. I closed my eyes and imagined him sitting next to me, healthy and happy.

I felt tears slip down my cheeks. I missed my best friend so much. If he was sitting beside me, he'd be teasing me right now. He often playfully poked at me during church, making it hard to remain reverent and quiet.

I could almost feel him lean over and whisper in my ear, his breath warm on my cheek. "My one finger is stronger than your whole body." I would ignore him, facing forward, pretending to listen to the speaker as I pressed down a smile.

Then he'd poke me and try to tickle me, anything to get a reaction as I tried my best to remain composed. Eventually I'd squirm and laugh, attracting looks

Christmas 2004 A church party, "A night in Jerusalem"

Summer 2004 Ellie and Rob

Summer 2003 Oregon Coast

from the people sitting around us, and rolled eyes from my kids.

But he wasn't sitting beside me, trying to disrupt my reverence. He was at home, sleeping. These days, that was all he did. He was rarely lucid and even when he was awake, he wasn't really himself.

During a church meeting, we were invited to bear our testimonies. One woman, Jenny Anderson walked up to the front of the room a little sheepishly.

"I don't know why I'm sharing this," she said with a soft smile. "But I feel like I should."

She told us how her kitchen had flooded twice. This time, the second time, the floors were ruined and needed to be replaced, again. She and her husband were trying to decide what type of floors to put in—tile or wood.

"We were especially worried about what type of floor would be best if the kitchen flooded again," she said. "I know it's silly, but we decided to pray about it and then we opened our scriptures and read the first thing we turned to."

She'd turned to a scripture about the strength of wood and decided wood floors it would be.

"I know that if you say a prayer and open your scriptures, your answer will be there," she said as she concluded her testimony.

Her words deeply affected me. I was struck by the simple truth of it and felt it was a direct answer to one of my deepest pleadings: *help me know what's going to happen.*

When I got home at 6:30 p.m., even though I was starving, I decided to go up to my room and pray, then open my scriptures. Sheri was downstairs feeding the

Summer 2000 Rob, Robbie and Jake

children and Rob was asleep. I was undisturbed as I knelt down and poured my heart out to God.

Then I grabbed my scriptures and flipped them open. The page before me was Alma 14, but the excerpt at the beginning of the chapter was cut off—the beginning sentence on the previous page—and the first thing I saw were the words: "*The prison walls are rent and fall. Amulek and Alma are delivered, and their persecutors are slain.*"

My heart soared. as I started reading, because I knew this story. I knew Alma and Amulek were delivered, so I knew my answer would be that Rob would be saved! When I reached verse 10, I stopped and sucked in a breath.

> *10 And when Amulek saw the pains of the women and children who were consuming in the fire, he also was pained; and he said unto Alma: How can we witness this awful scene? Therefore let us stretch forth our hands, and exercise the power of God which is in us, and save them from the flames.*

I realized I'd forgotten the first half of this story. The women and children are in pain. They were being put to death. Amulek is saying, "Hey, we need to save them!" But then Alma responds:

> *11 But Alma said unto him: The Spirit constraineth me that I must not stretch forth mine hand; for behold the Lord receiveth them up unto himself, in glory . . .*

What did this mean? I didn't remember this part of the story. I didn't remember anyone in pain and dying. What was the Lord trying to tell me? I kept reading through the rest of the chapter as Alma and Amulek are imprisoned and mocked because they couldn't save their own people. But even as it seems all hope is lost, their fate changes:

> *26 And Alma cried, saying: How long shall we suffer these great afflictions, O Lord? O Lord, give us strength according to our faith which is in Christ, even unto deliverance. And they broke the cords with which they were bound. . . .*
>
> *28 And Alma and Amulek came forth out of the prison, and they were not hurt; for the Lord had granted unto them power, according to their faith which was in Christ.*

I sat in shock as I pondered what I'd read. I thought to myself, *are you freaking kidding me*? How many chapters in the Book of Mormon involve people living and dying? But of all the chapters I could've turned to, I turn to the one with *both* situations happening. What was the Lord trying to tell me? That even though Rob is suffering, it's not in his fate to be saved? Or that if we persevere in our faith, eventually we will be freed from this trial? I really wasn't sure what to make of it.

Obviously the Lord doesn't want me to know yet because he gave me a chapter that presents both possibilities, I thought. *It is not yet time for me to know.*

"Which means I need to keep on fighting," I said to the empty room. Heavenly Father didn't want to give me a clear answer because I needed to keep coming to Him, searching my scriptures, and exercising my faith. He probably knew the second I was sure what He had in store for me, planning mode would kick in. I'd forget about going to Him for help because I'd be busy preparing for what was coming next.

There was still a chance I'd get the miracle I was desperate for.

CHAPTER 7

MARCH 2008

I will not leave you comfortless: I will come to you.

JOHN 14:18

We'd been playing a waiting game since Rob's first radiation treatment. The doctors couldn't do a scan on him until all the radiation left his body. Though I was stubbornly hopeful, I had no idea if the cancer had spread or not. But the time had finally come! The radiation was gone and a scan was scheduled. I was nervous and excited for his appointment on Monday that I didn't get much sleep the night before.

From the moment I woke up Monday morning, one thing after another went wrong. Rob was supposed to drink a special liquid to help his body show up on the scan, but he had thrush in his mouth and drinking was painful for him. Every time I held the liquid up to his mouth so he could swallow, he'd throw it back up. I prayed enough liquid got in him to do what it needed to do.

Jennifer's husband, Brian, helped me get Rob to the hospital. When we got there, it took the nurse half an hour to find a vein she could use to hook up Rob's IV because he was dehydrated. I could see the nurse and technician were getting frustrated as every attempt to get in the IV failed.

"Should we take off his shoe and see if there's a spot on his foot?" I said with a laugh, trying to lighten the mood.

"Well, we might need to call the doctor and see how important it is to get this scan," the technician said. "He's not in any shape to do the scan and he doesn't look like he's in any shape to do the chemo."

My mouth dropped open and my heart dropped to my feet. "No, we have to do the scan," I said. "We need it to know what kind of treatment should be done for his cancer." I resisted the urge to stomp my foot as I declared, "We're not leaving here until he gets the scan."

The technician eyed me, reading the determination written in every line of my body, and shrugged. "Okay."

The nurse finally found a workable vein and the IV was hooked up. Even though Rob was barely coherent, they got the scan done and told us the results would be

Skiing at Brighton 1995 Rob, me, JD and Tasha

Summer 2004 McCall, Idaho: Tasha, JD, me and Rob

out soon. When we got home, we had a changing of the guard as Sheri left and JD, my brother, and Sande, my mother, flew in.

When JD first went in to say hello to Rob, I could see the shock on his face at Rob's condition. "He looks like a person from a refugee camp," I overheard him say to my mother later.

I knew Rob looked bad, but what person going through radiation looked vibrant and healthy? Once the thrush went away, he could start eating more. Once the results of his scan came in, we could make a treatment plan. He'd be fine, I assured myself. Everything was going to be fine.

But the next day, I got the news: Rob's cancer had spread.

After two phone calls, one page, and a text message, Doctor Liss finally called me at three in the afternoon. She didn't waste time getting to the point. "In his gut area, where we did the original biopsy, there is more cancer. And in the lymph nodes under his left arm, there is more cancer. There's also a little nodule on his liver."

"Then let's schedule chemo for tomorrow," I told her urgently. I'd been hoping, fasting, and praying for better news, but I wasn't going to give up on him yet. I had enough faith, right? And with faith in Christ, all things are possible.

To my relief, she agreed to get him in for treatment that Wednesday.

JD kept my twins entertained while I was on the phone. He seemed charmed by them and I smiled whenever I heard their combined laughter as he chased them around or made up games to play with them.

"It's fun to watch twins interact with each other," JD said to me over dinner. "John was playing with a toy and Luke barged right over, sat on John and started playing with the toy. Most 17-month-old babies would've

Twins fighting

Summer 2008 me and the twins

screamed out and started crying, but John just leaned over to continue playing with his toy."

I nodded. "They really share a special bond." I didn't speak my next thought, but I added to myself that I was glad everything happening with their dad was going over their head. As far as Luke and John knew, they were just two lucky boys who had lots of visitors coming to play with them every day.

That night, Bishop Haymond and Brother Denfield stopped in to visit with me. The kids were excited and hyper to have JD and my mother over that the only quiet spot in the house was the twins' bedroom. They followed me in and I turned around and just stared at them, trying not to cry before anything was even said. Yesterday was hard but I'd still been full of hope. Today, I was barely hanging on.

Both the men standing across from me were shy and gentle; men with quiet strength and big hearts. Bishop Haymond was well aware of Rob's situation because all the church members who came by to help us kept him updated. The only thing he didn't know yet was the news I'd gotten today: that the cancer had spread.

When I filled him in on the latest details, he gently suggested it was time to let Rob be at peace. To let him enjoy whatever time he had left on earth.

"Don't make him do more chemo," the bishop said, his eyes sad, his voice soft. "Let him rest now."

I stared at him in shock for a moment. With all the disappointment and bad news I'd gotten today, THIS was the final straw. "Don't do chemo?" I said. More like roared. The words shot out of me with all the force of my shattered soul. I was holding on to the barest thread of hope and here this man, this man who was supposed to support me and guide me and *help* me, was taking a pair of scissors to it. How could he? How dare he?

"How dare you come into my house and tell me to let my husband die," I shouted. "I will fight for him. I won't give up on him and you can't make me."

"The chemo just kills the body," Bishop Haymond said quietly. "He's already weak. There's no way he'll survive. Do you really want to do that to him?"

Snip, snip, I felt the thread get cut in half and fall away. I screamed, I yelled. I was in such a rage that I can't even remember what I said, but I know it wasn't polite and it involved more harsh language than the bishop had ever heard from me before. He stood there, silent, his hands at his sides and his expression heartbroken. He didn't argue. He didn't tell me to stop. He just let me scream until my throat hurt and I went hoarse, until the tears were coming so hard and fast, I was choking on them.

When I finally stopped, heaving out exhausted breaths into the tense silence, he nodded. "Okay. Well, we just came by to check on you. Is there anything else we can do for you?"

I blinked, the rage clearing from my eyes. The room came into focus again, the anger that had swept through me subsided like an ocean wave retreating from the sand. I hugged my arms around myself and shook my head. "No. We're good. Thank you for asking."

After the bishop left, another church member and family friend, Casey Gosehart, came over to help care for Rob. When he was getting ready to leave, I stopped him at the door.

"The bishop told me not to give Rob more chemo," I said.

Casey lifted his eyebrows in surprise but didn't speak.

"We're told to accept council from our bishops," I continued. I blinked back tears and sniffed. "But I don't want to. What do I do?"

Casey sighed, leaning a shoulder against the front door. I knew he was the person to ask because Casey was no stranger to loss. Last year, he and his wife had lost one of their twins.

"The bishop counseled us from the Church of Jesus Christ of Latter-day Saints handbook to inter her after we told him of our desire to cremate," he said, referring to his deceased daughter. "Although Karen and I had not felt comfortable with burial, we took the matter before the Lord again. After much discussion and prayer, we decided cremation was still the best option for us."

I nodded with understanding and smiled with gratitude. As long as I listened to the bishop and seriously considered his council, I was being obedient. But that didn't mean I *had* to do what he said.

That night, March 5, I wrote on my blog:

> Today has been a difficult day for Rob. He talks very little and when he does, he's barely alert and confused. His mouth and throat are still hurting from the thrush, even though it's starting to clear up. I know right now it hurts to eat and even swallow for Rob.
>
> My brother gave Rob a blessing this morning and in it, he blessed Rob that the medicine would work

quickly so he could start eating more. He also blessed Rob that he would be able to talk to me and the kids.

Ellie and I went out tonight for some dessert and one-on-one time. I asked her how she was doing and how she felt about Daddy. If you know Ellie, you know I'm giving a very abridged answer: she misses Daddy playing and joking with her, but it's great having all the visitors! Rob's siblings and his dad are coming this weekend. I hope they are prepared to see him.

Tonight, we had all kinds of visitors. I felt comfort in their words that they shared with me. My mom was reading in the scriptures tonight and opened up to Ether, chapter 12. She was reading the chapter to me and verse 12 really struck home with me. **"For if there be no faith among the children of men, God can do no miracle among them."**

I can honestly say that I don't know what is going to happen. I know my Heavenly Father has a plan and I have complete trust in Him, I just don't know what the plan is yet. I do know I'm going to

May 2007 Rob and Ellie dancing

fight for Rob. Until the Lord lets me know otherwise, I'm going to fight! Like the poster in his room says, "Believe in Miracles & Fight the Battle!"

Love,
Patti

After posting my blog, I set about getting ready for the next day. I found the bustle—as I yelled for Ellie to put away her laundry and Robbie to make sure his backpack was cleaned out—familiar and comforting. My mother helped me set aside lunches for the next day and I asked the kids to set out clothes for school. We'd long ago learned mornings were too hectic to leave undone any task that could be done the night before.

But I paused mid-sandwich as I heard Rob's weak voice coming from the playroom. He was calling my name. I dropped the knife I was holding and rushed to his side.

"Rob, I'm here," I said, coming into the room. "What do you need?"

"A kiss," he said hoarsely.

I bent down and gave him a kiss, lingering for just a moment before pulling away. He smiled, then his eyes fluttered closed and he went back to sleep.

The next morning I woke up and realized that, for the first time in weeks, Rob and I had slept through the whole night! It was the best night's sleep I'd had in a long time. I yawned, stretched and leaned over to peek at Rob. He was still sleeping so I let him be and quietly crept out of the room and up the stairs to wake the children.

I got Ellie and Jake moving, but when I went in to wake Robbie, I found him sitting on his bed, his arms wrapped around his stomach. He looked up at me in the doorway, his eyes full of a deep sadness. "I don't want to go to school today," he said. "I don't feel good." I stared at him for a moment. I generally had a strict school attendance policy: if you're not bleeding, throwing up, or feverish, you go to school. Robbie knew this but he didn't try to feign a fever or act like he was going to throw up. He simply sat and stared at me, his shoulders slumped. He looked so sad, so broken.

I sighed and nodded. "Okay," I said, deciding to make an exception. "You can stay home. Tidy up your room. I've got to go get your dad ready for his doctor's appointment."

I left Robbie and headed downstairs, kissed Ellie and Jake before they headed out the door for their carpool, and went into the playroom, where Rob was still sleeping.

"Honey," I said, gently nudging my husband. I paused, but he didn't move. I frowned, and nudged a little harder. "Rob? Rob, wake up."

No response. I stood back up, my heart beginning to thud. Rob was often groggy and he slept a lot, but he'd never needed this much prodding to wake up before.

"JD!" I called out to my brother.

I told JD Rob wasn't waking up and let him make a few attempts. Still nothing. I left JD in the room to continue trying while I went to my phone to text Doctor Liss. It wasn't quite 9 a.m. yet, and I wasn't sure she'd welcome a phone call. *Rob's not waking up* was all I wrote.

I didn't feel much of anything. I'd been totally focused on getting Rob to his doctor's appointment that I was having a hard time recalibrating my brain. If he didn't wake up, could we still take him? I was glad he'd gotten good sleep last night, but it was time to wake up now. At this point, I was in total denial that Rob's current condition was scarier than anything else we'd been through.

Within minutes, Doctor Liss called me back. I quickly answered the phone and held it to my ear.

"This is it," she said, her voice sad but firm. "We need to call hospice right now. I'm heading over."

"What's hospice?" I asked her, confused.

"They'll come in and help you," she said. I could hear movement through the phone, as if she was opening and closing a door. "They'll bring in all the medical supplies you'll need and help you take care of Rob. It's either that or take him to the hospital and let them do it there."
"Oh," I said. I hated hospitals. They felt sterile and cold. They separated Rob from the kids. But hospice sounded like a great idea. They came in with the medical supplies we needed and took care of Rob in the home? Why weren't we doing this the whole time? "That sounds good. I'll call hospice."

I hung up with Doctor Liss, got on the phone with hospice and then went in to find JD still sitting by Rob, looking helpless. I filled him in on the new developments, my voice almost chipper. "Isn't that great?" I said. "Hospice will come in and take care of Rob for us. We won't have to go to the hospital! I wonder if they could do the chemo treatments that way, too."

"Patti," JD said.

Something in the way he spoke my name made me stop. "What?"

"Don't you know what hospice *is*?" he asked.

Wherefore Didst Thou Doubt?

"I—" I opened my mouth to answer but the way he was looking at me, I knew I'd gotten something wrong.

"Patti, he's not going to live through this," he said. "Hospice only comes when they aren't going to survive." I heard Doctor Liss' voice in my head then, loud and clear. I heard the words she'd first said to me when I answered the phone, words I'd somehow missed the meaning of at the time.

"This is it," she said.

This is it.

My hands dropped to my sides and I felt myself collapse internally, even though I was still standing on two feet. It registered somewhere in the back of my mind that JD had begun to sob. I might've been crying, too, I wasn't sure. I was lost somewhere deep inside myself, in a black void of shock as three words repeated and repeated until my conscious mind would finally admit the truth of them.

This is it. This is it. This is it.

And then I blinked as I realized Robbie was home. I needed to tell him.

Rob and Robbie at the ballpark

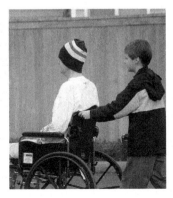

Robbie pushing Rob in his wheelchair

My body moved, taking the familiar path out of the playroom, up the stairs, down the hall, to the door of Robbie's room. My hand reached out to swing the door open. I wasn't fully aware of how I was doing it but somehow, I move forward, stepped into the room and stopped.

Robbie was still sitting on his bed, crumpled up like a puppet with its strings cut.

My voice came out but it sounded stiff and alien, too high pitched. "You need to go downstairs and be with your dad. He doesn't have much longer."

Robbie rose up and stared at me in shock. Then he jumped down and ran past me, screaming, "Daddy! No! You can't die! You can't die! Don't die, Daddy!"

Much later, I would remember when I fasted before Rob's last checkup. I hadn't fully understood the meaning of Alma, chapter 14. I knew the verses were about living and dying but I'd thought it was the Lord's way of not answering my question yet.

Rob loved baseball and loved watching his boys play.

After Rob's death, I realized how perfect that section of scripture was. Like Amulek, who was pained by the women and children being consumed by fire, I didn't want to see Rob suffer. I didn't want to "witness this awful scene". Yet I knew he was going to be safe with God, I knew the Lord would receive Rob "up unto himself, in glory". The second half of that chapter was God speaking to me and my family: even though our world was tumbling down; even though we were suffering great afflictions, God would deliver us.

But as I followed Robbie down the stairs, all I could think about was how I would let everyone else know . . . this was it.

CHAPTER 8

MARCH 2008

Behold, God is my salvation; I will trust, and not be afraid: for the Lord Jehovah is my strength and my song; he also is become my salvation.

ISAIAH 12:2

TEN YEARS EARLIER, IN 1998, Rob was sitting up in bed and pointing out a mole that was bleeding on his back. I was only 23 and unsure what a bleeding mole meant so I called his mom, a nurse, to ask about it. She suggested we visit a dermatologist.

The dermatologist cut it out and sent it in for testing. It turned out to be cancerous, so Rob went back in to have a huge circle around the area cut out. They went in almost an inch deep and even removed the lymph nodes.

My oldest son, Robbie, was barely two years old, and I was pregnant with my second, Jake. At this time, life was scary because I was a new mom, fresh out of college, and unsure what my future with a husband and two kids would look like. Cancer was a small thing, easily fixed in a few doctor appointments.

They told us the cancer had not spread. The following

Wherefore Didst Thou Doubt?

Summer 1998 Rob, Robbie and I at Andy and Jeni's wedding

spring, they declared him cancer free. Nine years after that, Rob was cleared to buy life insurance. Easy. Done.

What I wouldn't learn until ten years later after that first mole appeared, was that if even one tiny cancer cell is missed, it can metastasize and spread. When this happens, the patient is unlikely to survive.

Cancer was no longer a small thing. Now, Robbie was crying at his father's bedside. My brother JD was in the garage, arranging hospice care and calling family members. When my doorbell chimed, I went to answer it, wondering how such mundane tasks like greeting a visitor could suddenly require this much energy and willpower.

"What do you need today?" Jennifer asked as soon as I swung the door open.

"This is it," I told her. Saying those words felt like a betrayal, like I was giving up on Rob. I was barely holding myself together as I stared at my best friend, one hand on the doorknob, the other pressed to my chest as if I could hold my breaking heart together.

She stepped forward and embraced me, letting me collapse against her shoulder.

Then she got to work. She arranged for the twins to go stay with the Allens, a family friend. Rob's family had planned to visit that weekend; they were called and notified that they needed to come as soon as they could. Meanwhile, my mom cleaned the house and my brother fielded the flood of phone calls coming in.

My house was busy, hectic, full of people. My doorbell chimed, my phone rang, people came in and out in a rushing whirlwind of activity but I sat still, in my chair beside Rob's bed, holding his limp hand and crying.

Just after lunch, Doctor Liss arrived. During the whole process with Rob's cancer, Doctor Liss continually surprised me with how much care she showed us, with how generously she gave of her time. On this day, especially, I was grateful to her. She took Robbie, who was still shaking with devastation, and sat him down in our living room. For two hours, she talked to him. She answered all his questions about Rob's cancer and the treatments he'd received and all the medical aspects of this ordeal.

Robbie, at 11 years old, had a firm understanding of the plan of salvation. He knew he'd be with his dad again someday. But he needed help understanding the why's and how's of what had happened to his father's body. It was such a blessing that he was able to get all the answers he needed from a doctor.

Doctor Liss may not have been able to save Rob's life, but through that one conversation, she saved Robbie's.

When hospice came at 3:30 p.m., Doctor Liss explained everything to them. They'd arrived with grief counselors who had kits for the children to help them process Rob's impending death so when Ellie and Jake got home from school, they were told the news in a gentle, child-appropriate way.

When they heard, Ellie and Jake joined Robbie and me at Rob's bedside. We all stood there, crying. Someone suggested we sing to Rob and Ellie piped up with a primary favorite, "Families Can Be Together Forever". We all sang, our voices shaky, our cheeks wet, but the hope of the lyrics settled in and provided some small comfort to us.

Robbie as a missionary

> *I have a family here on earth. They are so good to me.*
> *I want to share my life with them through all eternity.*
> *Families can be together forever, through Heavenly*
>   *Father's plan.*
> *I always want to be with my own family, and the*
>   *Lord has shown me how I can.*
> *The Lord has shown me how I can.*
> *While I am in my early years, I'll prepare most carefully,*
> *So I can marry in God's temple for eternity.*
> *Families can be together forever, through Heavenly*
>   *Father's plan.*

PATTI EPPERSON

*I always want to be with my own family, and the
Lord has shown me how I can.
The Lord has shown me how I can.*[7]

I wasn't sure how much they understood of what was happening. It must've been very confusing for them. They were surrounded by family members that they loved. The kitchen was packed with snacks and treats that people had brought over. They were given grief processing coloring books to play with, so on the one hand, there were all these things to be excited about. But everyone around them was crying and they knew something bad was happening to their dad.

As the day wore on and news spread, our home filled with friends and family. They gathered in the playroom, around Rob's bed. We talked about Rob, shared favorite memories and laughed about all the good memories he'd been a part of.

By 9:30 p.m., Rob's family arrived at the airport and

May 2001 The Eppersons

Summer 2007 Rob's family

were shuttled to our house. Thankfully, our friends and neighbors, the Elliots, loaned us an RV that we parked in the driveway. We had Rob's four siblings, two parents, my brother, and other family members all staying with us at the moment—there was no way to fit them all inside.

When Rob's brothers, Andy, Rod, AJ, and Jimmy, along with Rob's parents, joined me at his bedside, Andy suggested we give Rob a blessing. I thought back to all the blessings we'd given him, blessings full of fervent hope that he'd somehow be healed. But not

July 2003 Oregon Coast Rob and his siblings: Rob, AJ, Jimmy, Erin and Andy

this blessing. This blessing would be one of comfort, to help Rob transition to the next world and my shattered heart broke a little more at the realization that this would be Rob's last blessing.

As Andy started the prayer, he had to choke back sobs. Though he was crying so hard he had to suck in breaths, the words came out clear. "You have all you need to see Jesus Christ and Heavenly Father," he told Rob. "You've been prepared so that you can be reunited with your family once again. You've honored your responsibilities as a father and you have been a faithful servant of the Lord."

My heart soared at these words. It was hard not to be upset that my time with Rob had been cut short. But I knew Rob had lived a good and honorable life. I knew when he had to face what was on the other side of the veil, he could do so with a clear conscience and triumphant heart.

Everyone stayed near Rob late into the night but a few people trickled out as the night wore on and they grew tired. The kids and I didn't leave Rob's side. We all crowded around the bed and turned on BYU TV to have something on in the background.

At 4 a.m., Rob's breathing became erratic. We gave him some pain medication to calm him.

A few hours later, as the sun was rising to signal a new day, Rob's breathing indicated he was in distress again. I looked at the clock. It was 6 a.m. I wasn't sure if I could give him more pain medicine this soon after the last dose, but when my brother, JD, came in to check on us, he offered to call hospice and find out how we could ease Rob's suffering.

Wherefore Didst Thou Doubt?

Summer 2007 Holiday Park Robbie, AJ and Rob

By the time JD returned to the room, twenty minutes later, Rob had really begun to struggle for breath. By now, the whole house was up and everyone had gathered around Rob. His brothers, his parents, his children, and I all stood, watching and waiting.

AJ, Rob's brother, was a 6 foot 2 inch cowboy, a huge guy with a shiny belt buckle and a couple of horses back home. He didn't normally inspire the word "gentle" when looking at him. But out of the quiet morning, his voice, as gentle, deep and melodic as any I'd ever heard, filled the room with this song:

> *"A poor, wayfaring man of grief*
> *Hath often crossed me on my way,*
> *Who sued so humbly for relief*
> *That I could never answer nay.*
> *I had not power to ask his name,*
> *Whereto he went, or whence he came;*

*Yet there was something in his eye
That won my love; I knew not why."*[8]

The spirit filled the room and though I didn't look to confirm it, I knew everyone was crying silently as we listened to the song. My eyes stayed on Rob's face, his sweet face childlike in his sleep. I gasped when I noticed, as AJ sang out the last line of the first verse, a tear roll down Rob's cheek. Even trapped in his body as he was, he could still be moved by the spirit.

When AJ finished singing, we all stood there in silence, waiting. For what, I didn't dare admit to myself.

Suddenly, Rob opened his eyes for the first time in 24 hours. I sucked in a breath and leaned forward, the barest glimmer of hope lighting in my chest. Maybe a miracle was still possible!

But as I leaned closer, I could see—there was nothing there. He was staring into space but his eyes were blank, empty.

Someone cried out, "No!" and I could hear the sniffling and sobs of everyone around me. I knew I was sobbing, too, but I felt disconnected from myself because my attention was fixed wholly on my husband.

He struggled for more air then stopped. Adrienne, his mother, reached over and gently closed his eyelids as he let out one last breath.

On March 6, 2008, at 6:25 a.m., Rob passed away.

We said our goodbyes, ushered the visitors out of the house, then I took Robbie, Jake, and Ellie upstairs to my bedroom. We'd DVR'd the Project Runway season finale—a favorite show in the Epperson home—so I queued it up and turned it on while the business of cleaning up my husband's lifeless body took place below us. I didn't want my kids to see the funeral home arrive. I didn't want them to see the men wheeling him out on a stretcher. They didn't need those memories.

At one point, I peeked out to see how everything was going and a family member asked me, "Why aren't you down there with Rob?"

"He's not there anymore," I said, my voice sounding hollow and far away to my own ears. "It's just a body."

The question stung a bit, but during this whole trial, I'd never left Rob's side. However, as soon as he took his last breath, I knew. He was gone. His body looked different without him in it. It just didn't *feel* like Rob anymore. I knew where I was supposed to be now—I needed to hold my babies close.

CHAPTER 9

MARCH 2008

It is your reaction to adversity, not the adversity itself, that determines how your life's story will develop.

PRESIDENT DIETER F. UCHTDORF[9]

IN THE NEW TESTAMENT book of Luke, there is a story about Jesus. Shortly after He was crucified, He appears in front of some of his disciples as they are traveling to a village. In Luke, chapter 24, verses 15 and 16, it says:

> *"And it came to pass, that, while they communed together and reasoned, Jesus himself drew near, and went with them.*
>
> *"But their eyes were* holden *that they should not know him."*

Because the disciples' eyes were holden, or blinded to the fact that they were walking with Jesus, he was able to talk with them and teach them. Sometimes, despite our faith and best efforts, we are too close to a situation to see it clearly.

For me, Rob's death was a total shock. Maybe I was the only one who didn't see it coming, but up until the morning he died, I truly believed he was going to live. I was shocked; I couldn't quite process what had just happened.

I thought I'd been doing everything right—praying, fasting, getting blessings, staying positive, doing whatever I could on my end to help Rob, and having faith that the Lord would take care of the rest.

We were good people. We lived good lives. We'd done nothing to deserve this . . . so why? Why had Rob been taken from me? As I sat on my bed, my children cuddled around me, Project Runway playing on the TV, my mind scrambled to make sense of what was going on. What was the value of my faith? What was its purpose? I'd believed wholeheartedly in the healing power of the Lord. I had no doubt that if He'd wanted to, He could've given us a miracle.

So why didn't He?

Then I remembered a few months earlier, when I'd been sitting beside a my good friend, Karen Gozart, just after one of her twins had passed away. She showed me a quote in her scriptures that had brought her comfort. In Doctrine and Covenants, Section 42, verse 48, it says: "And again, it shall come to pass that he that hath faith in me to be healed, *and is not appointed unto death*, shall be healed."

As I thought of this scripture, I realized, I'd never considered whether Rob was appointed unto death. And then I thought of when Jesus walked with his disciples on a long journey. He made it so they couldn't recognize Him so that He could teach them. It was only after He taught them that He revealed Himself.

I had a mountain of faith in the Lord. But if I'd known Rob was supposed to die, I would've given up. I would not

Trying to get a family picture! Feb. 2008

Rob and I

have spent all those nights searching my scriptures or praying and seeking comfort and help. During this trial, my faith had grown because of my diligent searching. Would I have searched this hard if I'd already known the ending?

Rob's death was part of the plan; part of the journey we were supposed to be on. Rob served as a missionary, not just for his family, but for everyone we came in contact with—at church, in our neighborhood, at the hospital. He sacrificed himself so that all of us could grow in our testimonies. I could almost hear him whispering the words to me: "I will go because it will help you and the kids, and everyone around us."

For the last three months, I thought I'd been working my hardest to take care of Rob. But it turned out, he'd been working to help me.

These truths didn't dawn on me all at once. They

came slowly as I worked through all the emotions related to grief.

As soon as Rob's body was removed, I found myself surrounded with people and questions.

"It's time to plan the funeral, Patti."

"What kind of casket should we pick, Patti?"

"Who's going to speak at the funeral, Patti?"

"What kind of flowers should we get for it, Patti?"

"What songs do you want us to sing there, Patti?"

I wanted to push everyone away and just scream at them to stop and leave me alone! I'd been totally unprepared for Rob's death; I was even less prepared to plan a funeral.

Rob's mom and my father came with me to the funeral home the day after Rob's death to pick out a casket. I walked into a room full of coffins and felt my stomach turn. I'd never imagined being tasked with such a

> Patti,
>
> I love you more than you could possibly imagine. Be good, and happy while I am away because someone loves you and is always thinking of how to make you happy.
>
> Rob

A note found under my bed about a month after Rob's death

June 9 1995 My dad and I

difficult decision at such a young age. And the options overwhelmed me. Did we want wood or black? Shiny or matte? Gold or silver detailing? Silk or satin lining? And don't forget to consider what kind of flowers you want so that they coordinate with the casket.

All I could think was *these are the stupidest questions ever!* My husband was gone, how could anybody expect me to think about flower arrangements at a time like this?

So I sat there and sobbed as Adrienne and my dad, sitting on either side of me, discussed the details over my head. Maybe at some future date, it would seem important to me that the flowers and the casket matched, but at *that* moment, I just didn't care.

As if planning one funeral wasn't stressful enough, I

had to plan two. Rob had grown up in Utah and had a large community out there, so I needed to hold one for everyone we knew in Washington, then move his body down to Utah. Only a week earlier, I'd been worried about traveling with a husband in a wheelchair. I'd never considered how much harder it would be to travel with a husband in a casket.

Through the haze of my grief, and with much help from friends and family, I managed to get everything planned. We held his Washington funeral on March 11 at a chapel in Battle Ground, Washington. The Utah funeral was held three days later, March 14, in American Fork, Utah.

For the music, I picked "Come Thou Font of Every Blessing" because it was one of Rob's favorites. A close family friend, Le Anne Bennett, rushed home to Washington from Europe so she could sing a solo of "Oh My Father" to the tune of "Come Thou Font of Every Blessing". I also picked "Come, Come Ye Saints" because Rob and I went on a pioneer trek a few years earlier and because of that, the song held special meaning for us. For

July 2005 Rob and I on a Pioneer Trek re-enactment

me, especially, it held meaning because I knew that many pioneers died on the journey west . . . and their families were fine and life went on. The world didn't stop spinning for them; it wouldn't stop spinning for me.

I spoke, along with Rob's brother, Andy, and my dad. I can't remember much of what I said, though I know I talked about the plan of salvation and my trust in the Lord and in the fact that we'd all be reunited with Rob someday.

My father's talk focused on the eternal promises made to us in the scriptures. He highlighted how painful the death of a loved one was, how inescapable it is, but how we can find hope in the Savior that we will all live again.

"Frequently, death comes as an intruder," he said. "It comes to a small little family and, to some, it makes us question life itself. It is an enemy that suddenly appears in the middle of life's wonderment, putting out light

Summer 2008 Griffith siblings: Janet, JD, Me, Josh, Kathy and Jordan

and placing a dark cloud over happiness. Death lays its heavy hand upon those dearest to us and at times leaves us baffled and wondering why. In certain situations, as in great suffering and illness, such as we have experienced, death comes as an angel of mercy. But for the most part we think of death as the enemy of human happiness, because our hearts ache so that we cannot fully understand the eternal reasons we are even here on this earth."

He quoted the book of John in the New Testament: "And yet our Savior, Jesus Christ, explained in the simplest terms when he said, 'And whosoever liveth and believeth in me shall never die' (John 11:25–26). This reassurance, this simple confirmation of a life beyond the grave, could well be the peace which was promised by the Savior when He assured his disciples: 'Peace I leave with you, my peace I give unto you: not as the world giveth, give I unto you. Let not your heart be troubled, neither let it be afraid' (John 14:27).

"'Ye believe in God, believe also in me. In my Father's house are many mansions: if it were not so, I would have told you. I go to prepare a place for you . . . that where I am, there ye may be also' (John 14:1–3). Our dear Rob is now absent of the pain of mortal life. Gone is the suffering of his sickness. He no longer has his frail body, but his spirit is strong and he will someday be reunited with a perfect body. He is again with loved ones, with a family who loved him while they lived. His spirit has gone to join theirs. And there will come that promised morning of the first resurrection, when he shall again take up his body and live in the arms of Patti, his dearest friend, his eternal companion, and enjoy the eternal love which bound them, which are the bonds of love, while they were mortal beings."

Andy, Rob's younger brother and best friend, recounted favorite memories from their childhood and painted a beautiful picture of Rob's life. But the thing that moved me the most was the poem he wrote and shared during his talk:

> *Dear Brother,*
> *Were you a volunteer? Did we all decide together*
> *Your life would be short, but someday last forever?*
> *Our hearts are aching now, our tears forever flow.*
> *The questions and confusion, someday I think we'll know.*
> *Dear Daddy*
> *Why did you leave? I needed you today.*
> *I lost my concentration in the first inning of play.*
> *Did you see me, Daddy, all dressed for the dance?*
> *I hope you could see, I hope you had the chance.*
> *We miss you, Daddy. We wanted you to stay.*
> *Dear companion,*
> *Forever is our claim, though time may separate.*
> *Someday I'll stand and wait for your hand to take me through the gate.*
> *Our promise is forever. Our children forever sealed.*
> *It won't be long, my love and hope. Forever keep me still.*
> *Dear Son,*
> *I know it doesn't seem fair, and you may not know why,*

*But you're the one I need, be still don't cry.
I gave you all you needed, I know you'd like to stay,
But I have missed you, too, my son. Here, come this way.*

At one point, I saw Jake's baseball coach, a tall, large man, hugging Jake and sobbing. It hit me how much Rob was loved, how many lives he touched. The speeches were beautiful and it was an emotional service. But when the pallbearers were carrying the casket out to the hearse, the beautiful, clear sky suddenly clouded over and rain burst down on their heads as they walked to the car, soaking the men. As soon as the coffin was loaded, the rain stopped.

"Typical Rob," Andy muttered. Everyone burst into laughter because it was true—if Rob was pulling strings in heaven, he would definitely use the opportunity to tease his family.

After the funeral, I wrote on the family blog:

What a wonderful day it has been. And just think we get to do it all over again on Friday! Just kidding!

I was amazed by the support of so many today. There were many people who drove down from Seattle and up from southern Oregon. Thank you very much! The service was beautiful. My father and Andy spoke. Andy will be speaking again in Utah. LeAnne Bennett sang and she'll sing again. Our church family is so amazing. They had everything taken care of! I can't even imagine how much time and effort went into making our day wonderful and stress free! I will post later my dad's and Andy's talks.

I know it will be hard. But I know Heavenly Father

would not bless me with this trial if I was not able to do it. I do trust in the Lord. This morning I was reading in Alma 31 and came across this scripture that I felt was perfect for me today. "O Lord, my heart is exceedingly sorrowful; wilt thou comfort my soul in Christ. O Lord, wilt thou grant unto me that I may have strength, that I may suffer with patience these afflictions which shall come upon me." I know I am strong because of everyone's prayers. I also am comforted though reading and studying the scriptures every day. This is where I can find peace, and feel close to Rob and my Savior.

Love,
Patti

One funeral was hard enough, but after that was done I had to go to Utah and do it all over again. Fortunately, so many family members came forth and took care of all the arrangements and details. I remember vaguely thinking, "I should be doing more to help," but it was all beyond me at the time. I couldn't see past my grief and shock enough to negotiate payments or make decisions about travel plans.

When we got to Utah, I was shocked at how many people came out. The funeral in Washington was packed with friends and family. Along with close friends and family, Rob's coworkers, his soccer team, our children's school friends and church members filled the pews. But they were all faces I knew well and expected to see.

Even though Rob hadn't been in Utah for more than five years, all the friends he'd made had not forgotten him.

Rob's uncle, Paul, spoke while Andy spoke again, and we used the same musical numbers. It was edifying to hear the same sweet stories about my husband again. At the end of the funeral, the man conducting the funeral, a man from Adrienne's congregation, spoke directly to Rob's brothers regarding their responsibility to their deceased brother's family.

"I would conclude with just this brief charge to these young Epperson brothers: we have a handcart that is out on the trail with miles yet to go to reach the Promised Land," Stake President Welch said. "I know that you know—Andy, AJ, Jimmy, and Rod—that there are going to be times with steep passes ahead. That there's going to need to be some help in pulling and pushing that handcart. I challenge you throughout the rest of your life, that you will define your love for this sweet brother by your willingness to be there at the side of the handcart as it reaches the Promised Land."

Later, on that blustery, cold day, Rob was buried in the American Fork Cemetery, less than a block from

Trial of Hope . . . Last Hill *by Al Rounds*

Jake, Ellie, me and Robbie

March 14, 2007 Rob's funeral

where Adrienne, his mother, lived. We joked that she couldn't have picked a closer spot unless it had been in her front yard. After the funeral, Adrienne often took walks down the street and over to Rob's grave. She tended it and took good care of it, making sure the gravestone was clear and neat.

We stayed in Utah for a full month after the funeral, and ended up moving there to be close to Rob's family later that summer, but I didn't often visit the cemetery. I appreciated that Adrienne tended it and kept it beautiful, but in my heart, I always remembered Luke, chapter 24, verse 5: "Why seek ye the living among the dead?"

I didn't need to visit Rob's grave, because I knew he wasn't there.

CHAPTER 10

Trust in the Lord with all thine heart; and lean not unto thine own understanding. In all thy ways acknowledge him, and he shall direct thy paths.

Proverbs 3:5–6

When I was young and still under the misconception that I had total control over my life, I had a whole list of things I'd never do.

- I'll never get married young.
- I'll never get married before I graduate from college.
- I'll never have kids before I graduate from college.
- I'll never be a single mother.
- I'll never live in Utah.
- I'll never go to work while I have young children at home.

One by one, every "I'll never" became an "I did."

I met Rob at Brigham Young University. We lived in the same apartment complex and his group of friends would always hang out with mine. When we met in September, we started dating immediately and he often teased me because I was still a teenager. By Christmas, I was beginning to panic. I really liked him, but I was only 19 and in Mormon culture, you date to marry. When you get a certain amount of serious about someone, you either get married or break up. I felt like the relationship was getting more serious than I meant it to be, so I told Rob we needed to take a break.

It was right before finals; I felt like a jerk, but it was on my list of "nevers"—don't get married young!

Shortly thereafter, I went out with another guy. I hadn't realized how effortless being with Rob was—how easy the conversation flowed, how natural it felt when he held my hand or put an arm around me. I spent my entire date with the other guy comparing him to Rob and thinking, *This is too much work! This is so dumb! What am I doing with him when all I can think about is Rob?*

Thank goodness Rob didn't give up on me! He could

January 1995 Rob and I at Sundance

Summer 1998 Holiday Park, Four generations of Robert Epperson

see that I needed space and he gave it to me, but after Christmas he invited me to go skiing with him and his two little brothers. I still remember so clearly sitting in the chairlift with one of his brothers while Rob rode up ahead with his other brother, Jimmy.

Jimmy was 11 at the time and I couldn't help noticing how Rob was so genuine and sweet with him as he helped him ski. And it was natural for Rob. That was just his personality—he took care of everyone around him. I remember thinking, *That's the man I want to be the father of my children.*

After the ski trip, I told Rob, "Okay, let's get married."

Rob looked at me in surprise. "Um. Okay."

In his eyes, I could do no wrong. Or at least, that's what he made me believe. We got married that June, when I was 20. My first and second "I'll never's" were erased, just like that.

In October, Rob's grandfather had a heart attack, which led to a serious surgery. Rob became upset by the idea that his children would never know his grandfather. This idea was painful for him because they'd always been very close.

"Patti," he said to me. "I want my kids to know my grandfather."

"Okay," I said. "We should have children then."

I got pregnant with Robbie right away and another "I'll never" fell away.

When Rob asked my dad for my hand in marriage, my dad made us promise him only one thing: that I'd graduate from college. But then I got pregnant and was looking at how to manage two college schedules with a newborn baby.

One day, I was driving through the BYU parking lot, half-panicked about some scheduling concern, and I cried out to Heavenly Father in my mind: *What have I done? I can't turn back now, I know that. But how am I going to do this!?*

April 1998 Brigham Young University graduation: me, Robbie and Rob

Then, as clear as if I was looking at a photograph, I saw Rob and I smiling as we stood in our graduation caps and gowns, a blond-haired little boy held up between us. It was weird—neither Rob nor I had blond hair and I was still early enough in my pregnancy that no gender had been revealed. But after that, I knew—we were going to have a little boy with blond hair. And everything was going to be okay.

Somehow every semester, the night before classes started, our schedules would fall into place: babysitters, classes, money. It was always at the last minute, but it always worked out. I never let myself get too stressed out in the moments in between because I knew: the Lord will show you little glimpses to help you along. It can be hard—when you're in the thick of it—not to stress and worry. But we were blessed and I couldn't ignore that.

Spring 2007 Rob and I

Summer 2007 Our family

We never had to pay for a sitter. Rob's sister or our friends were always willing to help us care for Robbie. Rob managed to work full time and go to school full time; I went to school full time and worked part time.

Through our efforts and with some help from the Lord, we managed to graduate on schedule: Rob with a Bachelor of Arts degree, me with a Bachelor of Science.

Even though the things I said I'd never do happened, I didn't have to give up on my dreams because of it.

But surely, the rest of the list was within my control. I knew I'd never divorce Rob. I knew he'd always take care of us. I was living a good and righteous life and that meant I would get to raise my children in a whole and intact family. Because when it came down to it, that was all I'd ever wanted. A normal, happy family.

But then my husband died.

I'd never seen that coming. I'd never thought to put

"I'll never be a widow" on my list. I honestly believed that by living a righteous life and making the correct choices, I could avoid all the pain and trials I saw the people around me dealing with. I was wrong, of course. Pain and suffering come to the best, the brightest, the most innocent of us. Why would it pass by me?

While I was still in Utah, shortly after the funeral, I went to sign the life insurance papers. The same day, Rob's company, Diamond Wireless, came and presented me with a huge check of donated work hours from his co-workers. A flood of money was coming in to help pay for the hospital bills and the funeral, but I wasn't joyful. I didn't want money—I wanted Rob.

I yelled out in the empty car, "Why!? Why, Lord? Why did you do this? We did everything we were told to do—we got married young, we didn't put off having a family. I still graduated college. I did everything by the book. I kept every commandment. I did everything you asked. Why did you take him away?"

I was crying so hard, I had to pull over. But suddenly, all these memories came flooding into my mind. Beautiful memories of Rob, of my family, of the kindness of everyone around us. Memories of being prompted to start a family early, to buy life insurance, to get out of debt. And as if someone were sitting beside me, I heard the whispered words: *Because you were obedient, you were blessed.*

I realized the blessings didn't come to prevent my trials. They came to help me deal with them. My mind began to re-route. Because we started a family early, I was blessed with five beautiful children before Rob died. Because we got out of debt, I would still get to stay home with the kids. Because I'd gotten my degree, if I did need to work, I'd be able to. Because we were kind to our neighbors and did lots of service, we were surrounded by friends in our time of need.

The blessing I'd wanted was for Rob to live. Because I was intently focused on that, it took me awhile to see all the other blessings I'd received instead.

It wasn't easy to work through these feelings, to see the blessings in spite of the pain and loss. Despite that, I tried my best to help my children along on their journey of grief.

I remember on the Saturday after Rob died, his friends had been planning to fly out and see him. They'd already booked and paid for their hotel in downtown Portland. Instead of cancelling the reservation, they offered it to me. I'd finished planning everything for Rob's funeral; there was nothing left for me to do. So I grabbed Rob's sister, Erin, my sister-in-law, Jeri, and Ellie and headed out for a weekend away. It was a surreal experience. At one point, while I was walking down the hotel corridor, I felt certain Rob was there beside me. That night we rented "27

Salt Lake City Temple June 9, 1995

Dresses" but I slept through it because, for the first time in days, I was finally able to sleep.

The next day, we went to Nordstrom for lunch. This was a familiar tradition to Ellie. It's one Rob had grown up with and something he'd passed along to his own kids. It was achingly comforting and it gave me a good chance to spend some time with Ellie, to talk about her thoughts and feelings. She understood that she'd see her father again someday but I don't think she'd quite realized how much her life was going to change now.

But a few nights later, Ellie and I were lying in bed and talking. She asked me all kinds of questions that a 7 year old going on 16 would ask: what was it like to get married in the temple? What was it like to *be* married? I told her that even though Daddy was gone, he and I were still married. Because we'd gotten married in the temple, we'd promised to be together for time and all eternity.

In that moment, it struck me as sad to imagine what it would be like to be married only "until death do us part." With Rob passing away, that would've meant we weren't married anymore.

I was happy for that bit of comfort. It was bad enough to lose him, but if that had been the end of

Summer 2008 Ellie and I

our marriage on top of it, I don't know how I would've handled it. But I knew we were still wedded. He was still my best friend and my first love. He was still the father of my children and I knew he was watching over our family.

When we were in Utah for the second funeral, we buried Rob on a Friday. Jake, who was 8 years old, came up to me the following Sunday and asked, "Where's Daddy?"

Surprised and heartbroken by his question, I said, "Jake. We just buried him."

Jake frowned. "I know. But Jesus was resurrected in three days and it's been three days. So where's Daddy?"

"He *will be* resurrected. I promise you," I said, sniffing back tears. "He will. Not right now. It won't be for awhile. But he will, just like Jesus was. And he'll be whole. He'll be able to run and play again, and wrestle with you."

Suddenly I was reminded of a talk I'd heard by Elder Joseph B. Wirthlin. In it, he said, "Each of us will have our own Fridays—those days when the universe itself seems shattered and the shards of our world lie littered about us in pieces. We all will experience those broken times when it seems we can never be put together again. We will all have our Fridays. But I testify to you in the name of the One who conquered death—Sunday will come. In the

Holiday Park: Rob and Jake

darkness of our sorrow, Sunday will come. No matter our desperation, no matter our grief, Sunday will come. In this life or the next, Sunday will come."[10]

So I told Jake, "Don't worry. Sunday will come."

Shortly after this conversation, I decided

McCall, Idaho Jake and Rob

I needed to move my now-fractured family to Utah at the end of the school year. I explained my reasoning on my blog on March 22:

> *Faith is taking that step into the darkness and knowing that the Lord will be with you, even though you*

February 2008 Rob and Jake

don't know how it will turn out. You need to step in the darkness.

I, too many times, want to see the end of the road or where it is going, but that is not how it works. When I get back home, I'm going to start getting my house ready to sell. At this time, I feel I need to be around family. My children need their uncles and aunts in their lives. I will take my step into the darkness and start this process.

The one thing I do know, is I have no idea where it's going. But the Lord has always been there for me. He has always blessed me and put me on the correct path. Again in my mind, things will go smoothly. I will sell my house, quickly move down here, and find a house with no problems. I am hopefully smart enough to know by now, that it will most likely not happen that way, but the way that it will happen, will be the Lord's way. Too many times, I have seen people force their will upon the Lord and they lose so many blessings. I hope not to make that same mistake. Trust in the Lord and He will lead (notice it is not the word "force:) you to paths of righteousness.

Love,
Patti

CHAPTER 11

Keep your chin up, trust in God, and believe in good things to come.

ELDER JEFFREY R. HOLLAND[11]

THE WHIRLWIND OF ROB'S sickness, death, funeral, and my subsequent move to Utah calmed down and by the end of summer, we settled into our new normal: a Utah family headed by a single mother. Life was busy with five kids but it was also lonelier than I could've ever imagined.

Though my days were full from the moment I woke up until I went to bed, a vast void followed me around, threatening to swallow me whole every time I stopped for a moment. Could this be worse than getting divorced, I wondered? Rob and I both came from divorced parents and I knew how much it hurt when a marriage failed and you were a single parent, but . . . at least they were still

Labor Day Weekend 2009 Jake, John, Ellie, Robbie, Luke and me

Easter 2008 Robbie, John, Ellie, Jake, and Luke

there somewhere. At least there was another human alive who loved and cared for your children, and was as invested in their well-being as you. Someone you could go to with questions or issues about the kids.

I'd been careful to avoid an unhealthy marriage, but I'd never thought to imagine what life would be like as a young widow.

Moving to Utah had been hard but necessary. I was surrounded by Rob's family and a wonderful new congregation. They were always willing to do whatever they could to help me. They surrounded and embraced us at this time and I appreciated all their efforts on our behalf.

Yet, there was a giant, Rob-shaped hole in our lives that no one could ever fill. Five kids is a big group and while people were willing to help when they could, they had families of their own. There was this awkward balance of trying to get help when I needed it, while still being considerate of the fact that my friends and family had families of their own. I was very careful not to take advantage. Which meant I never really got a break. No downtime, no true rest, and no one that I could completely lean on. My best friend, my confidante, my support system and the love of my life was now gone.

And I was weary.

Through life insurance and generous donations from friends and family, plus the sale of our home in Washington, I had enough money to continue staying at home for the time being. But I needed to have a plan for the future. I knew I'd have to get a job eventually.

When we were living in Washington, I would go to Institute classes every Thursday morning. It was one of my favorite parts of the week. Knowing this, my brother, JD did some research and approached me with an idea: why don't I teach Institute?

The idea intrigued me. Currently, I had my kids and nothing else. Nothing in my life that was *mine.* I discovered

Summer 2009 McCall, Idaho

that if I was part of the Church Education System (CES) for two years, it would qualify me to go back to my alma mater, Brigham Young University, to get a masters degree in religion. Working as an Institute teacher would definitely qualify.

"If I taught Institute for two years," I told JD, "I could apply to BYU right about the time the twins would be old enough to go to school full time."

I spoke to my bishop and told him my idea; along with the hopes and plans of my heart. He agreed and a weekly Institute class was set up. I'd done something for myself on my own. I'd taken my first big step toward creating my own future.

Even with this bit of hope on the horizon, settling into a routine was hard and I found myself yelling at the kids more than I wanted to. It's not like they never frustrated me in the past, but before, I could glance at the clock, take a deep breath, and count down the hours until Rob got home from work. But now, glancing at the clock only reminded me how slowly time passed. There was no countdown because no one was coming home to help me.

One especially rough day, I was yelling at the kids to clean up and they were ignoring me. I glanced at the clock to do the Rob countdown and remembered with a jolt that he wouldn't be home any time soon. I told Ellie to keep an eye on the twins and went up to my room.

I grabbed my scriptures and shut myself in my closet. Through tears of frustration and loneliness, I poured out my heart to my Heavenly Father.

"I can't do this," I whispered to Him. "I can't do this. How can I do this? What am I supposed to do?"

As I finished my prayer and sniffed back my tears, I opened my scriptures. The first words I saw shocked me.

"For when they saw your conduct, they would not believe in my words." (Alma 39:11)

I blinked at the page a few times. "Seriously!?" I cried out. "I'm dying here. I can't even breathe and this is the scripture you're giving me?"

I read and re-read the words, letting them sink in. The truth hurt but I wouldn't turn from it. Heavenly Father was reprimanding me. He knew I was stretched thin, that I was in pain and suffering, but He still wanted me to understand: I couldn't act this way. I couldn't take out my hurt and loneliness on my children.

And then another thought entered my mind, a gentle reminder. When I married Rob, I made a covenant to obey and listen to him. I realized I still had a husband I could ask for help, another person who very much cared about the welfare of our children. I'd never thought about it before—but I could ask him for help.

This thought brought forth another one: there was another person very much invested in the welfare of all His children. I could ask Heavenly Father for His help. In the scriptures, it says to put your burden on Christ.

I tried to remember the last time I'd offered up such a heartfelt pleading for help. While Rob was sick, I was on my knees countless times but once all of that had settled down, I think I forgot to keep seeking the Lord's help.

I knew I needed to depend on the Lord to get me through Rob's sickness and death. But was He still here, willing to help me in these small moments?

I was ready to admit to myself that I couldn't raise

John John

these kids on my own. I literally couldn't. I knew I needed to spend every day praying and pleading with the Lord, asking for his help and putting my burdens on Him. There was no other option for me.

I needed His help because I wasn't a good enough mom on my own.

This was a turning point for me. I knew I'd been failing as a single mother and I kept thinking I needed to get my act together, do better, be more. But the Lord never intended me to be a superhero or a perfect mother. He never expected me to truly do it alone.

He really is there, no matter the situation. At this point, it shouldn't have been hard for me to depend on Him, yet I found myself forgetting and waiting until there was no other option.

I should've known better! Just go to the Lord *first* instead of as a last resort!

Elder Jeffrey R. Holland said, "Every one of us has times when we need to know things will get better . . . For emotional health and spiritual stamina, everyone needs to be able to look forward to some respite, to something pleasant and renewing and hopeful, whether that blessing be near at hand or still some distance ahead. It is enough just to know we can get there, that however measured or far away, there is the promise of 'good things to come.'"[12]

Life slowly got easier. There were many dark days after Rob's death when I felt like my struggles were more than I could bear, but my testimony of Christ's enabling power was a fire within me that had been stoked and strengthened so much that even at my worst moments, it never blew out.

This is what saved me. This is the one reason I was okay after Rob died.

As I've studied the scriptures in the aftermath of all I went through, I noticed that continually, prophets depended on the Lord and were blessed with miracles: Abraham, Joseph of Egypt, Moses, the Apostles—there are many examples of miracles that came through unyielding faith. Why are we told these stories? Why were they important enough to put in the Bible, to be passed down for thousands of years? It's because God

me

is the same now as He was then; He's the same yesterday, today, and forever. He wants us to know that what He did for them, He'll do for us.

Why do we, a society rich with blessings and miracles, have such a hard time believing that? I think it's because miracles don't look the same as they used to. Someone could look at my life and see only the trials and none of the blessings, but I can testify that there were countless miracles as Rob and I walked that path together. The family and friends who came to serve us, the doctors who fought for us, the time we got to spend together, and the eternal lessons we learned as a family.

What we went through is not that different than those in the days of the Bible. It's a modern example of deliverance and help just as God delivered the children of Israel from Egypt.

I remember hearing a talk where the speaker said to the youth in the church, "Would you go to school without putting your pants on?" This garnered a laugh from the audience because of course not! Can you imagine anything more horrifying as a teenager? That's the stuff of nightmares. And yet, what's more important than clothing is putting on the mantle of God. We must pray and read our scriptures every day, otherwise we're going out into this tumultuous world unarmed. The Lord loves all of us and He wants to help us. But because He gave us the gift of free will, He can't intervene unless we invite Him to.

Eventually, I was blessed to meet a good man who was willing to join his family with mine. I got the chance to remarry and add new children to my family. My children were given the gift of another earthly father. I was able to tour the world, speaking about the faith-building experience of Rob's cancer.

Now, ten years later, I can look back and see all the blessings, great and small; all the miracles big and little, that have brought me here. It's hard to know when you're in your closet, crying your eyes out, that better days are ahead—and that's where faith comes in.

In Romans 8:28, we are told that "in all things God works for the good of those who love him." In the Mormon religion, we talk a lot about the principle of compensation, which promises us that we will be compensated for every loss we suffer. It may not come right away or in the way we expect, but it will come. I had the worst thing that I could ever imagine happen to me, and I'm okay. I'm okay because of the Lord's help, because I depended on Him.

We are told to be humble like a child and what's more humbling than trusting the loving parent who knows better than you? As we grow up, we begin to think we know everything, but as little children, we look up to our parents and the adults in charge of us and we trust them completely.

I learned through my trials to trust in the Lord completely and now I understand better why we're instructed to be like little children. It's not easy—especially when you can't see the light at the end of the tunnel. But I promise it's there. I stand as a witness that the principle of compensation is true. I wouldn't be where I am today without my Savior.

I know these principles look different for everybody. My ending is different than other people's. Some will have the miracle where their loved one is healed. That wasn't my miracle. My miracle is that I'm okay. My kids are amazing. And I was able to find happiness again.

I still was a single mom for almost two years. I still had to get married again. I still struggled. It was not all a cake walk and it didn't all turn out perfectly. But I choose to look at the blessings and that's why I can now stand as a witness.

Go to the Lord, no matter what your problem is. Know that He is there for you. It doesn't have to be a major trial. It doesn't have to seem serious in the eyes of the world. If it matters to you, it matters to Him. Trusting in the Lord's plan for your life is hard but I can promise that if you do, it will all work out.

> *"Some blessings come soon, some come late, and some don't come until heaven; but for those who embrace the gospel of Jesus Christ, they come."*
>
> JEFFERY R. HOLLAND[13]

When Joseph Smith was imprisoned in Liberty Jail, it was one of the darkest times in his life. Yet, by depending on the Lord for strength, comfort and understanding, he was still able to grow spiritually during those months. In the wonderful talk, "Lessons from Liberty Jail: A Prison and a Temple," Elder Jeffrey R. Holland spoke about how everyone can grow and become stronger during life's hardest trials.

During a blessing I received while dealing with Rob's cancer, I was counseled to read Doctrine and Covenants, sections 121, 122, and 123. These were the sections on Liberty Jail. As I read, one scripture stuck out to me the most. D&C 121, verse 9 says: "Thy friends do stand by thee, and they shall hail thee again with warm hearts and friendly hands."

I was extremely blessed to have so many friends and family members willing to help me through my trial with Rob. There was no way I could've done it alone.

Rob's aunt, Cathy Howard knows Al Rounds, the artist who painted this depiction of Liberty Jail. On the morning that I called to tell Adrienne that the end was near for Rob, Cathy happened to be at her home with this painting. When Cathy woke up that day, she felt prompted to be at her sister, Adrienne's house. Thank goodness Cathy was there! Adrienne needed her support to get flights ready and to be by her side as Adrienne prepared to watch her son pass away.

This painting holds such a special place in my heart because I know—even in the hardest of times—we can grow and become closer to Christ. I'm grateful to Al Rounds for giving us permission to use depictions of two of his paintings, which are dear and personal to me, in this book.

ENDNOTES

1. Dallin H. Oaks, "Opposition in All Things," 186th Annual General Conference of the Church of Jesus Christ of Latter Day Saints, April 2016.

2. Thomas S. Monson, "I Will Not Fail Thee, Nor Forsake Thee," 183rd Semiannual General Conference of the Church of Jesus Christ of Latter Day Saints, October 2013.

3. Richard G. Scott, "Trust in the Lord," 165th Semiannual General Conference of the Church of Jesus Christ of Latter Day Saints, October 1995.

4. David A. Bednar, "Bear Up Their Burdens with Ease," 184th Annual General Conference of the Church of Jesus Christ of Latter Day Saints, April 2014.

5. Spencer W. Kimball, *Teachings of the Presidents of the Church: Spencer W. Kimball*, 2006, pg 79-88.

6. Dennis E. Simmons, "But If Not...," 174th Annual General Conference of the Church of Jesus Christ of Latter Day Saints, April 2004.

7. Ruth Muir Gardner, *Families Can Be Together Forever, Children's Songbook*, current-1989, pg 188.

8. James Montgomery, *A Poor Wayfaring Man of Grief, Hymnal*, current-1985, Hymn #29.

9. Dieter F. Uchtdorf, "Your Happily Ever After," 180th Annual General Conference of the Church of Jesus Christ of Latter Day Saints, April 2010.

10. Joseph B. Wirthlin, "Sunday Will Come," 176th Semiannual General Conference of the Church of Jesus Christ of Latter Day Saints, October 2006.

11. Jeffrey R. Holland, "An High Priest of Good Things to Come," 169th Semiannual General Conference of the Church of Jesus Christ of Latter Day Saints, October 1999.

12. Jeffrey R. Holland, "An High Priest of Good Things to Come," 169th Semiannual General Conference of the Church of Jesus Christ of Latter Day Saints, October 1999.

13. Jeffrey R. Holland, "An High Priest of Good Things to Come," 169th Semiannual General Conference of the Church of Jesus Christ of Latter Day Saints, October 1999.

ACKNOWLEDGMENTS

There is no possible way this book could have come to pass without the help of many people! First, my dad, John Griffith. You planted the seed in my mind and helped me get started. You knew I could do this, even when I thought I couldn't. My brother, Bishop/Dr. JD Griffith. You not only encouraged me to start teaching institute, but got me speaking to youth all over the world (Malaysia makes me an international speaker)! You saw me as someone who could help others, even while I was still growing myself. All my friends from Battle Ground. This book will never do justice to the great amount of service and Christlike love you all gave our family. In fact, all my family and friends over the past ten years who helped us—I can't name you all here but your names are written in my heart forever. Your service, love and friendship mean so much to me.

My institute class: for six years, all who attended taught me each and every class! My knowledge and testimony of the gospel grew as I taught from the scriptures each and every week. I love and miss you all! Angela Hextell, for encouraging me while eating Mexican food that I could actually do it. Crystal Liechty, you laughed and cried with me! You helped me more than you can even imagine. You listened to the spirit when I couldn't hear the answer. Seriously, without you, there would be no photos at all!

Or a book, for that matter! You have helped me through the jungle of the publishing/book creating world with very little harm. Kristy G. Stewart, I am truly sorry for ruining your holidays. Thank you for being patient with me. You helped the book look exactly how I imagined! Amy Stoddard, for making me believe I am the funniest person you know. My kids, who have put up with me stressing out and being a mean mom. Steve Jorgensen, you encouraged me, no, you actually *made* me, write this book. Without Steve's love and support, this book would never have come to pass.

Made in the USA
Columbia, SC
09 February 2018